THE KEY
STUDENT STUDY GUIDE

Science 9 Applied

THE KEY student study guide is designed to help students achieve in school. The content in each study guide is 100% curriculum aligned and serves as an excellent source of material for review and practice. To create this book, teachers, curriculum specialists, and assessment experts have worked closely to develop the instructional pieces that explain each of the key concepts for the course. The practice questions and sample tests have detailed solutions that show problem-solving methods, highlight concepts that are likely to be tested, and point out potential sources of errors. **THE KEY** is a complete guide to be used by students throughout the school year for reviewing and understanding course content, and to prepare for assessments.

Published 2008
Copyright © 2008 Castle Rock Research Corporation

Rao,Gautam,1961 –
THE KEY – Science 9 Applied (2009 Edition) Ontario

1. Science – Juvenile Literature. I. Title

Castle Rock Research Corporation
2340 Manulife Place
10180 – 101 Street
Edmonton, AB T5J 3S4

1 2 3 FP 10 09 08

Printed in Canada

Publisher
Gautam Rao

Contributors
Ken Boyko
Susan Cairns
William Day
Jared MacLeod
Susan Oreski
Maureen Orr
Kara Went

Dedicated to the memory of Dr. V. S. Rao

THE KEY— Science 9 Applied

THE KEY consists of the following sections:

KEY Tips for Being Successful at School gives examples of study and review strategies. It includes information about learning styles, study schedules, and note taking for test preparation.

Class Focus includes a unit on each area of the curriculum. Units are divided into sections, each focusing on one of the specific expectations, or main ideas, that students must learn about in that unit. Examples, definitions, and visuals help to explain each main idea. Practice questions on the main ideas are also included. At the end of each unit is a test on the important ideas covered. The practice questions and unit tests help students identify areas they know and those they need to study more. They can also be used as preparation for tests and quizzes. Most questions are of average difficulty, though some are easy and some are hard—the harder questions are called *Challenger Questions*. Each unit is prefaced by a **Table of Correlations**, which correlates questions in the unit (and in the practice tests at the end of the book) to the specific curriculum expectations. Answers and solutions are found at the end of each unit.

KEY Strategies for Success on Tests helps students get ready for tests. It shows students different types of questions they might see, word clues to look for when reading them, and hints for answering them.

Practice Tests includes one to two tests based on the entire course. They are very similar to the format and level of difficulty that students may encounter on final tests. In some regions, these tests may be reprinted versions of official tests, or reflect the same difficulty levels and formats as official versions. This gives students the chance to practice using real-world examples. Answers and complete solutions are provided at the end of the section.

For the complete curriculum document (including specific expectations along with examples and sample problems),
http://www.edu.gov.on.ca/eng/curriculum/secondary/science910curr.pdf.

THE KEY *Study Guides* are available for many courses. Check www.castlerockresearch.com for a complete listing of books available for your area.

For information about any of our resources or services, please call Castle Rock Research at (905)625-3332 or visit our website at http://www.castlerockresearch.com.

At Castle Rock Research, we strive to produce an error-free resource. If you should find an error, please contact us so that future editions can be corrected.

CONTENTS

Success at School

KEY FACTORS CONTRIBUTING TO SCHOOL SUCCESS

In addition to learning the contents of your courses, there are some other things that you can do to help you do your best at school. Some of these strategies are listed below.

- **ATTEND SCHOOL REGULARLY** so you do not miss any classes, notes, or important activities that will help you learn.

- **KEEP A POSITIVE ATTITUDE.** Always reflect on what you can already do and what you already know.

- **BE PREPARED TO LEARN.** Have the necessary materials (pencils, pens, notebooks, and other required materials) with you in class.

- **COMPLETE ALL OF YOUR ASSIGNMENTS.** Do your best to finish all of your assignments. Even if you know the material well, practice will reinforce your knowledge. If an assignment or question is difficult for you, work through it as far as you can so your teacher can see exactly where you are having difficulty.

- **SET SMALL GOALS** for yourself when you are learning new material. For example, when learning formulas, do not try to learn everything in one night. Work on only one formula each study session. When you understand one particular formula and have memorized it, move on to another one. Continue this process until you have learned and memorized all of the required formulas.

- **REVIEW YOUR CLASSROOM WORK** regularly at home to be sure you understand the material you learned in class.

- **ASK YOUR TEACHER FOR HELP** when you do not understand something or when you are having difficulty completing your assignments.

- **GET PLENTY OF REST AND EXERCISE.** Concentrating in class is hard work. It is important to be well-rested and have time to relax and socialize with your friends. This helps you to keep a positive attitude about your school work.

- **EAT HEALTHY MEALS.** A balanced diet keeps you healthy and gives you the energy you need for studying at school and at home.

HOW TO FIND YOUR LEARNING STYLE

Every student has a certain manner in which it seems easier for him or her to learn. The manner in which you learn best is called your learning style. By knowing your learning style, you can increase your success at school. Most students use a combination of learning styles.

Do you know what type of learner you are? Read the following descriptions. Which of these common learning styles do you use most often?

- **Do you need to say things out loud?** You may learn best by saying, hearing, and seeing words. You are probably really good at memorizing dates, places, names, and facts. To learn the steps in a process, a formula, or the actions that lead up to a significant event, you may need **to write them and then read them out loud**.

- **Do you need to read or see things?** You may learn best by looking at and working with pictures. You are probably really good at puzzles, imagining things, and reading maps and charts. You may need to use strategies like **mind mapping and webbing** to organize your information and study notes.

- **Do you need to draw or write things down?** You may learn best by touching, moving, and figuring things out using manipulatives. You are probably really good at physical activities and learning through movement. You may need to **draw your finger over a diagram** to remember it, *tap out* **the steps** needed to solve a problem, or *feel* **yourself writing** or typing a formula.

SCHEDULING STUDY TIME

You should review your class notes regularly to be sure you have a clear understanding of all the new material you learned. Reviewing your lessons on a regular basis helps you to learn and remember ideas and concepts. It also reduces the quantity of material you need to study prior to a test. Creating a study schedule will help you to make the best use of your time.

Regardless of the type of study schedule you use, you may want to consider the following strategies for making the most of your study time and effort:

- Organize your work so you begin with the most challenging material first.
- Divide the subject content into small, manageable chunks.
- Alternate regularly between your different subjects and types of study activities in order to maintain your interest and motivation.
- Make a daily list with the headings *must do*, *should do*, and *could do*.
- Begin each study session by quickly reviewing what you studied the day before.
- Maintain your usual routine of eating, sleeping, and exercising to help you concentrate better for extended periods of time.

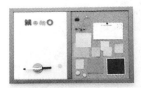

CREATING STUDY NOTES

MIND-MAPPING OR WEBBING

- Use the key words, ideas, or concepts from your class notes to create a *mind map* or *mind web*, which is a diagram or visual representation of the given information. A mind map or web is sometimes referred to as a *knowledge map*.

- Write the key word, concept, theory, or formula in the centre of your page.

- Write down related facts, ideas, events, and information and then link them to the central concept.

- The following examples of a Frayer Model illustrate how this technique can be used to study scientific vocabulary.

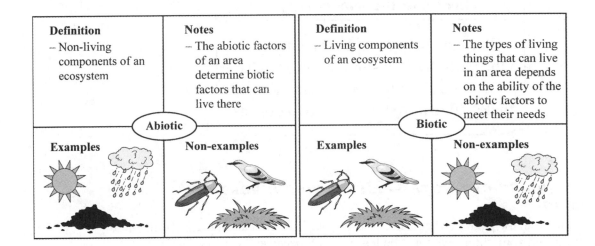

INDEX CARDS

To use index cards while studying, follow these steps:

- Write a key word or question on one side of an index card.
- On the other side, write the definition of the word, answer to the question, or any other important information you want to remember.

> **What is the difference between heat and thermal energy?**

> **What is the difference between heat and thermal energy?**
>
> Thermal energy is the total energy of the particles in a solid, liquid, or gas. Heat is the amount of the thermal energy that is transferred between two objects.

SYMBOLS AND STICKY NOTES—IDENTIFYING IMPORTANT INFORMATION

- Use symbols to mark your class notes. For example, an exclamation mark (!) might be used to point out something that must be learned well because it is a very important idea. A question mark (?) may highlight something you are not certain about, and a diamond (◊) or asterisk (*) could mark interesting information you want to remember.
- Use sticky notes to mark a page in a book that contains an important diagram, formula, or explanation.

KEY STRATEGIES FOR REVIEWING

Reviewing textbook material, class notes, and handouts should be an ongoing activity. Spending time reviewing becomes more critical when you are preparing for tests. You may find some of the following review strategies useful when studying during your scheduled study time.

• Before reviewing a unit, note the headings, charts, graphs, and chapter questions.

• Highlight mathematical key concepts, vocabulary, definitions, and formulas.

• Carefully read over each step in a procedure.

• Draw a picture or diagram to help make the concept clearer.

KEY STRATEGIES FOR SUCCESS—A CHECKLIST

Review, review, review: that is a huge part of doing well at school and preparing for tests. Below is a checklist for you to keep track of how many suggested strategies for success you use. Read each question and then put a check mark (✓) in the correct column. Look at the questions for which you have checked the *No* column. Think about how you might try using some of these strategies to help you do your best at school.

KEY Strategies for Success	Yes	No
Do you attend school regularly?		
Do you know your personal learning style—how you learn best?		
Do you spend 15 to 30 minutes each day reviewing your notes?		
Do you study in a quiet place at home?		
Do you clearly mark the most important ideas in your study notes?		
Do you use sticky notes to mark texts and research books?		
Do you practice answering multiple-choice and written-response questions?		
Do you ask your teacher for help when you need it?		
Do you maintain a healthy diet and sleep routine?		
Do you participate in regular physical activity?		

Reproduction

Biology: Reproduction - Processes and Applications

Table of Correlations

	Specific Expectation	Practice Questions	Unit Test Questions
9.1.1	Understanding Basic Concepts		
9.1.1.1	*describe the basic process of cell division, including what happens to the cell membrane and the contents of the nucleus*	1a, 1b, 2, 3	1
9.1.1.3	*demonstrate an understanding that the nucleus of a cell contains genetic information and determines cellular processes*	6, 7	4
9.1.1.4	*describe various types of asexual reproduction that occur in plant species or in animal species and various methods for the asexual propagation of plants*	8, 9, 10	5
9.1.1.5	*describe the various types of sexual reproduction that occur in plants and in animals, and identify some plants and animals, including hermaphrodites, that exhibit this type of reproduction*	11, 12	6, 7
9.1.1.6	*compare sexual and asexual reproduction*	13, 14, 15	8
9.1.1.7	*explain signs of pregnancy in humans and describe the major stages of human development from conception to early infancy*	16, 17, 18	9
9.1.1.2	*demonstrate an understanding of the importance of cell division to the growth and reproduction of an organism*	4, 5	2, 3
9.1.3	Relating Science to Technology, Society, and the Environment		
9.1.3.1	*describe the use of reproductive technologies in a workplace environment and explain the costs and benefits of using such technologies*	21	12
9.1.3.3	*identify local environmental factors and individual choices that may lead to a change in a cell's genetic information or an organism's development, and investigate the consequences such factors and choices have on human development*	23, 24	
9.1.3.4	*provide examples of the impact of developments in reproductive biology on global and local food production, populations, the spread of disease, and the environment*	25, 26	13
9.1.3.5	*describe careers that involve some aspect of reproductive biology*	27	14
9.1.3.2	*examine some Canadian contributions to research and technological development in the field of genetics and reproductive biology*	22	
9.1.2	Developing Skills of Inquiry and Communication		
9.1.2.1a	*through investigations and applications of basic concepts: - identify a current problem or concern relating to plant or animal reproduction*	19	15
9.1.2.1b	*- formulate scientific questions about the problem or concern, and develop a plan to answer these questions*		
9.1.2.1d	*- select and integrate information from various sources, including electronic and print resources, community resources, and personally collected data, to answer the questions chosen*		
9.1.2.1e	*- organize, record, and analyse the information gathered*		
9.1.2.1f	*- predict the value of a variable by interpolating or extrapolating from graphical data*		
9.1.2.1g	*- communicate scientific ideas, procedures, results, and conclusions using appropriate language and formats*		
9.1.2.1h	*- defend orally a position on the concern or problem investigated*		
9.1.2.2	*use a microscope to observe and identify (in living tissue and prepared slides) animal and vegetable cells in different stages of mitosis, as well as cells undergoing asexual reproduction*	20	11
9.1.2.3	*design and conduct an investigation into the stages of cell division to determine changes taking place in the nucleus and cell membrane*		

Specific Expectation		Practice Questions	Unit Test Questions
9.1.2.1c	*- demonstrate the skills required to plan and conduct an inquiry into reproduction, using instruments and tools safely, accurately, and effectively*		10

9.1.1.1 *describe the basic process of cell division, including what happens to the cell membrane and the contents of the nucleus*

9.1.1.2 *demonstrate an understanding of the importance of cell division to the growth and reproduction of an organism*

During cell division a parent cell divides to produce two offspring cells. The chromosomes of each offspring cell are identical to the chromosomes of the parent cell. There are three distinct stages in the division of a cell. It is important to learn what takes place during each stage and how this affects the growth and reproduction of an entire organism.

STAGES OF CELL DIVISION

1. Interphase
   - is the first stage of cell division.
   - is the longest stage—a cell spends about 90% of its life cycle in this stage.
   - dividing cell produces nucleic acid and proteins that are used in growth and cell repair.
   - replication of DNA occurs, and copies of organelles such as
   - mitochondria, chloroplasts, ribosomes, and nuclei are produced.

   a. Mitosis
      - cell prepares to divide into two identical daughter cells that are copies of the original parent cell.
      - mitosis is a process of cell division that involves four short phases: prophase, metaphase, anaphase, and telophase.

   b. Prophase
      - duplicated chromosomes coil up into X-shaped chromosomes and migrate to each pole of the cells, where they attach to **spindle fibres**.

   c. Metaphase
      - the spindle fibres line up along the centre of the cell.

   d. Anaphase
      - the X-shaped chromosomes are pulled apart resulting in two sets of identical chromosomes moving to opposite poles of the cell.

   e. Telophase
      - the spindle fibres are absorbed, and the cell is ready to divide.

f. Cytokinesis
– is the final stage of the process. The cytoplasm divides, the cell membrane fuses together, and two daughter cells are formed.

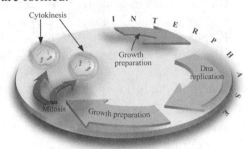

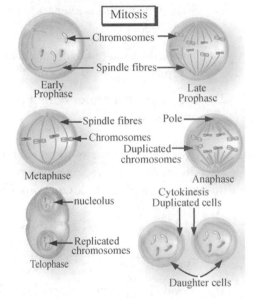

Mitosis

Chromosomes

Spindle fibres

Early Prophase

Late Prophase

Spindle fibres   Pole

Chromosomes

Duplicated chromosomes

Metaphase   Anaphase

Cytokinesis
Duplicated cells

nucleolus

Replicated chromosomes

Telophase

Daughter cells

Cytokinesis

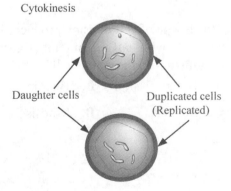

Daughter cells   Duplicated cells (Replicated)

1. cell cycle
2. mitosis
3. cytokinesis

A cell does not live forever. During the cell's life span it grows and changes. Different cells have different life spans. In general, plant cells live 10 to 30 hours. Animal cells live 18 to 24 hours. It is therefore important that cell reproduction occurs continually. Cell reproduction is required for growth and repair.

When DNA in the nucleus is not properly replicated, which sometimes happens, cell division can become uncontrolled. Both the growth and ability of a cell to reproduce can be harmed, resulting in a mutation or cancer.

Practice

Use the following information to answer the next multipart question.

1. There are two main types of cell division in living organisms. Cell division plays many roles during the life span of organisms, both plants and animals.

Part A

Open Response

What is the main purpose of the two types of cell division, mitosis and meiosis?

(2 marks)

_____
_____
_____
_____
_____
_____
_____
_____

Part B

Open Response

Describe four roles of mitosis.

(4 marks)

_____

_____

_____

_____

_____

_____

_____

Use the following information to answer the next question.

The given figure illustrates a particular stage of meiosis.

2. The stage depicted in the given figure is

   A. anaphase I   **B.** telophase I

   C. anaphase II   **D.** telophase II

Use the following information to answer the next question.

Mitosis is the type of cell division that maintains the original number of chromosomes in daughter cells. It starts with prophase and ends with telophase. Prophase is preceded by interphase, while telophase is succeeded by interphase.

3. Which of the following statements is **true** about interphase?

   A. The nuclear membrane breaks down during interphase.

   B. Sister chromatids are separated during interphase.

   C. The replication of DNA occurs during interphase.

   D. Chromatin condenses during interphase.

4. The liver has the capacity to regenerate after an injury. This regeneration occurs through which of the following processes?

   A. Mitosis

   B. Meiosis

   C. Zygote formation

   D. Blood circulation

5. Which type of cell division produces two new cells with half the amount of genetic information as the parent cell?

   A. Binary fission   **B.** Budding

   C. Meiosis   **D.** Mitosis

9.1.1.3 *demonstrate an understanding that the nucleus of a cell contains genetic information and determines cellular processes*

NUCLEUS

All teams have leaders that help the team achieve goals. Leaders organize, delegate duties, and make important decisions to help the team survive. Plants and animals cells have an organelle that acts as a team leader and controls the function of the cells. The leader or decision maker of each cell is its **nucleus**. It too is made of parts that work together to ensure the cell performs the job required of it. Each cell has specific duties as part of a function like breathing or digestion. These cells form tissues, such as the lining of the stomach, and these specialized tissues form parts of different organs, for example, the stomach. Organs are grouped into systems, such as the digestive system. All of the organism's systems work together to perform processes necessary for survival. The **nucleus** is a part of each cell and provides the decision making for cell specialization. Observe the diagrams below of an animal and plant cell.

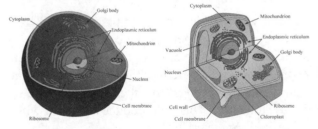

Plant and animal cells are similar, although there are differences. See if you can spot them. Generally speaking, each cell is a separate entity filled with a cytoplasm, a jelly-like substance that is home to several tiny organs called **organelles**.

The **nucleus** is an organelle that controls the activities of all the cell parts. It has a nuclear membrane, which separates and protects it, and a **nucleolus**, which makes ribosomes, essentially carriers of messages. The master set of instructions as to what a cell is supposed to do is contained in just two molecules within the nucleus. These molecules, shaped like a spiral staircase, are called deoxyribonucleic acid or DNA. When a cell is ready to divide, the strands of DNA coil up into compact X-shaped structures called **chromosomes**.

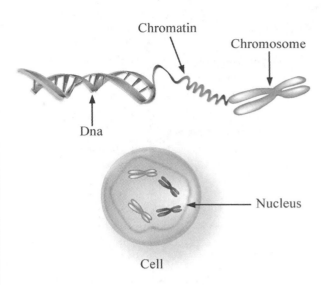

Chromosomes come in pairs. In humans 46 chromosomes are arranged in 23 pairs, but other organisms have different numbers of chromosomes. On each chromosome are parts called **genes**. They are the producers of proteins that determine what the cells will become and how they will function. Proteins can be enzymes or hormones that affect the processes taking place in the organism. The nucleus of the cell regulates protein production so that DNA bases match up properly during cell division, otherwise mutations can occur. Mutations can and do affect cell function and growth.

Use the following information to answer the next question.

A typical plant cell is made up of several main structures.

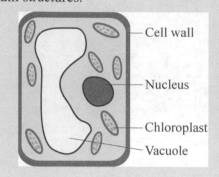

- Cell wall
- Nucleus
- Chloroplast
- Vacuole

6. In which of these organelles is DNA found?

A. Chloroplast   **B.** Cell wall

C. Vacuole   **D.** Nucleus

7. The reason the nucleus can control cell activities is that it contains

A. a gelatinous matrix

B. the genetic material

C. the other cell organelles

D. the powerhouses of the cell

9.1.1.4 *describe various types of asexual reproduction that occur in plant species or in animal species and various methods for the asexual propagation of plants*

ASEXUAL REPRODUCTION

Many common plants are **clones**, that is, they are exact copies of a parent plant. Almost all single-celled organisms are also identical to a parent cell. This duplication of organisms occurs through a process called **asexual reproduction** in which only one parent is needed to produce an offspring, called a **daughter cell**.

Cloning occurs naturally in nature and can also be human assisted. Bioengineers try to reproduce plants with useful characteristics, such as resistance to pests or drought. They also clone bacteria that can be used to fight diseases.

There are many types of **asexual reproduction**. These include **binary fission**, **budding**, **fragmentation**, **vegetative reproduction**, and **spores**. Organisms use asexual reproduction to try to increase their species' chance of survival. The amoeba is an example of a single-celled organism that is very low on the food chain and is food for other predators. Using asexual reproduction of the type know as **binary fission**, the amoeba can quickly and in great numbers enhance its chances for survival. One cell replicates and divides into two cells, two cells into four, and so on.

Other single-celled organisms can reproduce themselves by **budding**, which involves growing a bud, attached to the mother cell, which contains an exact copy of its genetic material. The bud can remain attached or will detach, depending on the amount of food and other nutrients available in its environment. Budding is common in some sponges and hydra.

You may have heard that with some starfish, such as the sea star, a portion of the starfish can regrow into an entirely new starfish. When part of an animal or plant can regrow into an identical copy of the parent, this type of asexual reproduction is called **fragmentation**.

Vegetative reproduction, used by plants such as the potato, occurs when special cells divide repeatedly to become clones of the original. When several desired characteristics are found on different plant varieties, cuttings from these plants can be grafted together. This will produce one plant with all desired characteristics.

Another method of asexual reproduction is called **spore formation**. In this method, lightweight, tough group of identical cells is produced by the parent and released to be carried by wind, water, or animals to locations where they may flourish if conditions are correct. Mushrooms commonly reproduce this way.

Use the following information to answer the next question.

8. Which of the following biological processes is depicted in the diagram?

    A. Budding

    B. Syngamy

    C. Neurogenesis

    D. Parthenogenesis

Use the following information to answer the next question.

A structure of proliferating cells develops from the body surface of the parent individual. This structure grows in size and forms a new individual that ultimately separates from the parent to lead an independent life.

9. The type of reproduction described is

    A. budding

    B. binary fission

    C. fragmentation

    D. multiple fission

Open Response

10. Why does asexual reproduction in hydra produce only identical offspring?

    _____

    _____

    _____

    _____

    _____

    _____

    _____

    _____

9.1.1.5 *describe the various types of sexual reproduction that occur in plants and in animals, and identify some plants and animals, including hermaphrodites, that exhibit this type of reproduction*

SEXUAL REPRODUCTION

When only one parent is needed to produce offspring, it is called asexual reproduction. Two parents of the same species, one male and one female, are needed to reproduce **sexually**.

Sexual reproduction leads to **genetic diversity** in offspring because **gametes** from both parents are mixed with each other. Sometimes, the genetic diversity is visible, as with height or skin colour but it can also be invisible, for example, having weak bones or poor eyesight. The random mixing and matching of DNA from the chromosomes of each parent creates altered combinations and therefore new characteristics within the new organism. Genetic diversity can result in an organism that is better able to adapt to its environment and thereby live to reproduce itself.

A good example is found in flowering plants. One with a strong fragrance is more likely to be fertilized by insects or animals, giving it a better chance of surviving and reproducing. Negative qualities such as taking a long time to mature enough to produce seeds can lead to less fertilization and therefore less chance of reproduction. Sexual reproduction can work both ways.

THE THREE STAGES OF SEXUAL REPRODUCTION

There are three stages of sexual reproduction: mating, fertilization, and development.

Mating happens when male and female gametes meet. This can happen externally, called **external fertilization**, in which the male and female gametes are expelled from each parent into the environment where they meet by chance. Sea urchins and some fish reproduce by sending out sperm and eggs and hoping they will meet up in their aquatic environment. Variables such as the time the eggs and sperm were released, the temperature of the water, and the presence of predators can affect the success rate of this type of sexual reproduction. To counter this risk, thousands of sperm and egg cells are released. Also, external fertilization does not require the time and energy needed to find a willing mate, nor are the new organisms in competition with the parents for nutrients. Unfortunately, fertilization is not guaranteed, and parents are not around to protect their young from predators who will eat little ones before they reach the age at which they can reproduce.

Internal fertilization requires sperm cells to be deposited inside of a female's body where they can meet an egg cell. One sperm cell among the millions that are deposited is allowed to penetrate the egg to insure that just one set of male chromosomes unites with one set of female chromosomes. The developing **embryo** is protected and nourished within the womb. The parent even stays around after birth to educate and protect the offspring, leading to a greater survival rate.

Disadvantages of internal fertilization include extra energy needed to find a mate and after birth nurturing while producing fewer babies.

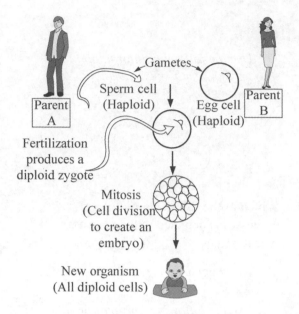

To understand the diagram above, it is necessary to be familiar with the terms **haploid**, **diploid**, and **zygote**. Human cells have two sets of 23 chromosomes. This is their **diploid** number (2×23). Each parent, male and female, contributes half their chromosomes (23). This is their **haploid** number, found in the sperm cell and again in the egg cell. Together, the sperm and egg combine to create 2×23 chromosomes, or a **diploid zygote**. The zygote undergoes **mitosis**, or cell division, to create an **embryo** and eventually a new organism with 2×23 chromosomes per cell.

The process to create **gametes** with half the number of chromosomes as body cells is called **meiosis**. Without meiosis, the joining of the sperm and the egg cell would produce an offspring with twice the number of chromosomes as its parents. Cell division occurs twice in **meiosis**, which results in the shuffling of genetic information and variation in the zygote produced. DNA is taken from each parent cell to produce a combination of both of them (containing 2×23 chromosomes).

Some organisms, such as earthworms and a few snails, as well as flowering plants, have both male and female reproductive organs. They are called **hermaphrodites** and can self-fertilize to create a zygote, embryo, and an entire new organism.

Practice

11. The process that involves the temporary union of two parents of the same species in order to exchange the male pronuclei is referred to as

A. syngamy   B. conjugation

C. plasmotomy   D. fragmentation

12. The process of uniting two dissimilar gametes to form a zygote is known as fertilization. Which of the following animal groups is correctly matched with the type of fertilization it exhibits?

A.

Animal	Fertilization
Frog	Self-fertilization

B.

Animal	Fertilization
Tapeworm	Cross-fertilization

C.

Animal	Fertilization
Earthworm	External fertilization

D.

Animal	Fertilization
Moose	Internal fertilization

9.1.1.6 *compare sexual and asexual reproduction*

COMPARING SEXUAL & ASEXUAL REPRODUCTION

Looking at the pros and cons of asexual reproduction, on the positive side, asexual reproduction results in the ability to produce huge numbers of offspring very quickly. As previously mentioned, this is a great advantage when a species is attacked or put into an unhealthy environment. Some members of the colony will usually survive. It also provides an advantage in the competition for available nutrients. In a short span of time, innumerable new cells are produced, so a limited amount of energy is expended in reproducing, and no time or energy is wasted searching for a desirable mate.

On the negative side, asexual reproduction is best suited for simpler organisms rather than large, complex, multicellular organisms. This makes the single-celled species more vulnerable to a negative mutation when replication of DNA is occurring. Another disadvantage is that entire populations can be wiped out if environmental conditions turn bad or there is an attack from a predator. Think how an entire colony of bacteria can be wiped out with just a small dose of antibiotics.

Sexual reproduction has the advantage of involving genetic information from two parents. As a result, there is much more variation. The recombination of genes leads to a better chance of the offspring surviving unfavourable conditions. The strengths of both parents emerge in the offspring. The major disadvantage of sexual reproduction is that it takes considerable time and vast amounts of energy to produce a single offspring. The parents are both usually found nurturing the young long after it is born, again using up energy. Sexual reproduction is a long process, and this limits the number of offspring produced.

Practice

13. Which of the following statements **best** explains the difference between asexual and sexual reproduction?

A. Asexual reproduction requires a fertilization process, while sexual reproduction does not.

B. Asexual reproduction involves only one parent, while sexual reproduction involves two parents.

C. Asexual reproduction involves two parents, while sexual reproduction involves only one parent.

D. Asexual reproduction requires a wet environment, while sexual reproduction requires a dry environment.

14. What is the **main** advantage of sexual reproduction?

   A. It only requires a single parent.

   B. It reduces the chromosome count of the offspring.

   C. It is less time consuming than asexual reproduction.

   D. It leads to offspring that are genetically different from the parents.

Open Response
---

15. What are the main disadvantages of asexual reproduction?

   _____

   _____

   _____

   _____

   _____

   _____

   _____

   _____

9.1.1.7 *explain signs of pregnancy in humans and describe the major stages of human development from conception to early infancy*

HUMAN DEVELOPMENT FROM CONCEPTION TO INFANCY

Scientists have broken down the stages of **embryonic development**. This refers to the growth and changes in an embryo as time passes. The first week after fertilization, the zygote goes through cell division to form a simple ball of cells called a **morula**. By the end of the second week, these cells have begun to specialize. This is called the **blastula** stage. These **embryotic stem cells** can develop into any type of cell in the body, so they are used in research and often examined and compared to insure normal development is occurring. Research is being carried out to determine if stem cells can be used to treat a variety of medical conditions in humans.

Following embryonic development is the **fetal stage**. During the growth of the fetus, over 38 weeks, cells **differentiate**, or become specialized. Some cells develop into skin tissues, some into organs, and some into nerves and enzymes.

Fetal development is divided into three stages, called **trimesters**. Each stage features certain changes. By week twelve, the end of the first trimester, the embryo has become a fetus. Organs and systems and nerves can be identified. During the second trimester (months 4 through 6), the fetus grows up to 35 cm and its weight increases to about two-thirds of a kilogram. Mothers can feel their babies moving. The third trimester (month 7 through 9), features further growth in size (40–50 cm) with exceptional growth in the brain and the formation of fat so that at birth the fetus is more or less ready to meet the outside world.

Use the following information to answer the next question.

In sexual reproduction, the gamete from each parent contributes half of the genetic material required to create an offspring.

16. During which of the following processes is the genetic material from two gametes combined to form a zygote?

   A. Blastula formation

   B. Morula formation

   C. Fertilization

   D. Fetal stage

17. When listed in the correct order, the stages of embryonic development are

    A. zygote → fertilization → morula → blastula

    B. fertilization → zygote → morula → blastula

    C. fertilization → morula → zygote → blastula

    D. blastula → fertilization → morula → zygote

Open Response

18. Briefly describe the following stages of embryonic development.

Zygote—

Morula—

Blastula—

_____

_____

_____

_____

_____

9.1.2.1a *through investigations and applications of basic concepts: - identify a current problem or concern relating to plant or animal reproduction*

CONCERNS IN REPRODUCTION

Problems relating to the reproduction of animals or plants usually result in a change in the natural pattern. Most often, two outcomes arise: either a population becomes too numerous and poses environmental problems, or the species comes close to extinction, which is both a serious loss and a change in the balance of the ecosystem in which the species existed.

A number of examples are provided for you to consider and research further.

EURASIAN MILFOIL

Milfoil is an aquatic plant that is native to Asia, North Africa, and Europe. It was brought to N. America as a decorative aquarium plant and was released into North American waters. Milfoil spreads quickly and can crowd out native plants in freshwater lakes. Because pieces of the plant can grow into mature specimens, it only takes a piece of milfoil on a boat propeller to spread the plant from one lake to another. This form of asexual reproduction allows this invasive plant to move into lakes where it was previously unknown and disrupt the normal ecology of the infested lakes.

Eurasian milfoil

PEREGRINE FALCON

The Peregrine falcon led a normal existence until human beings started using the chemical DDT as a pesticide. The chemical remained in the bodies of prey animals and accumulated in the falcons as they continued to eat the prey. The chemical caused the thinning of egg shells due to a disruption in the deposition of calcium in the shells. Many young falcons died before hatching because the egg was too fragile to survive.

Peregrine falcon

ALGAE BLOOMS

Bodies of freshwater can become clogged with excess algae plants. These algae blooms are caused by excess chemicals getting into the water, particularly phosphorous. Algae need these chemicals in order to grow and reproduce. In natural water systems, the chemicals are found in limited supplies, which in turn serves to limit the amount of algae that can grow. If humans allow untreated soaps or excess fertilizers to reach the water, the algae respond and overpopulate the water. Besides blocking sunlight for other plants, some algae produce toxins that can have a devastating effect on both aquatic animals and land-dwelling animals that visit the water to drink.

Algae bloom

HYBRID SPECIES

Sometimes, two separate species that do not normally interbreed are able to produce offspring that live. These offspring possess a mixture of the traits of the two parents, but they may not be fertile themselves. Although rare, if this process happens in nature, it can be thought of as part of the process of speciation, the creation of a new species. Often, however, hybrid species are brought about through the actions of humans intentionally trying to mix species to create fanciful offspring. This may involve the use of artificial insemination, in which case the creation of the offspring is completely artificial and not the result of the chance mating of two species.

LIGERS AND TIGONS

Ligers are born from a cross between a male lion and a female tiger. Tigons are the opposite, where the female mother is a lion and the male father is a tiger.

ZORSE

Crossbreeding between a horse and a zebra results in a zorse being born.

PIZZLIES AND GROLARS

Grizzly bears and polar bears normally do not encounter each other because of geography and habitat. They simply do not live in the same regions. These sorts of crosses have always been brought about with the interference of humans and usually involves mating between the two species when they are found in the same zoo. A hybrid bear was found in the wild in 2006, the first time a natural cross between these two species was detected outside of a zoo.

CAMA

The hybrid offspring of a cross between a camel and a llama is called a cama. The natural breeding of Camas is impossible due to both the massive size difference between the two parents and other natural mechanisms designed to prevent this kind of crossbreeding. The only way to create a cama is through artificial insemination of the mother.

Practice

Use the following information to answer the next question.

Monoculture is a type of agriculture in which only one type of crop is grown over successive years.

19. Which of the following impacts is monoculture **most likely** to have on the natural environment over many years?

   A. Increase in crop production

   B. Decrease in flora diversity

   C. Increase in soil fertility

   D. Decrease in soil fauna

9.1.2.1b - *formulate scientific questions about the problem or concern, and develop a plan to answer these questions*

FORMULATING SCIENTIFIC QUESTIONS

Asking the right questions in science is very important, because the questions you ask determine what kind of answers you are going to get.

DO YOU HAVE THE TIME?

A young man, rushing off to work, is asked by a passerby, "Do you have the time?". He replies, "Yes, I do," and continues walking. While the passerby might expect the man to provide the time as part of his response, technically he does answer the question. Maybe a more precise request would have helped. "What is the time, please?" is a question to which the only suitable response is to provide the time, which is the information that is wanted.

Questions in science can be like this example in some ways. Often, a specific answer is what is wanted, but you cannot get specific answers by asking general questions.

WHAT KILLED THE COW?

Mr. Brown has a herd of cows on land that has a river running through it. He starts to notice that a few of his cows are dying, and he needs to find out why. His suspicions are aroused by the pulp mill upstream. He thinks that the mill is dumping waste into the water that the cows drink. He orders water testing to be done.

Essentially, Mr. Brown has already asked a question. Rather than asking a very general question, "What killed the cows?", he has formed a hypothesis that he can test. "Did wastewater from the mill kill the cow?" By investigating one factor he can determine if he is on the right track.

The results from the tests show no unusual levels of any chemicals in the water except for unusually high levels of phosphates and nitrates. The local agricultural advisor from the provincial government told Mr. Brown that he is likely overfertilizing his land and suggested a visit to help Mr. Brown with his problems. During the visit, the advisor notices a dugout with pristine clear blue water in it. "Do the cows ever drink from the dugout," he asked. Mr. Brown admitted that they did, but that the runoff from the mill does not go into the dugout. The advisor asked Mr. Brown if he ever had algae problems in the dugout. He was suspicious because excess fertilizers could also run off from the fields and cause an algae bloom in the water. "Yes," he said, "but I have solved that problem by coppering the dugout." The addition of copper sulfate to the water did kill the algae, but Mr. Brown did not know how to calculate the correct amount to add and ended up dumping too much copper sulfate into the water. Further testing revealed that Mr. Brown's cows were suffering from copper poisoning that was affecting their nervous systems.

Every hypothesis asks a question that can be tested. Often, researchers think they know the answer to the question before they even conduct the tests. Like in the case of Mr. Brown's cows, the results can sometimes surprise and lead to new questions being asked. With enough scientific inquiry, most problems can eventually be solved.

9.1.2.1c - *demonstrate the skills required to plan and conduct an inquiry into reproduction, using instruments and tools safely, accurately, and effectively*

INQUIRY INTO REPRODUCTION

The basis for reproduction of any kind is the ability of single cells to reproduce. In this way, an entire organism can be obtained from a single fertilized egg cell. Mitosis is the cell division process that creates two daughter cells that are identical to the original cell.

To observe evidence of mitosis, it is necessary to use a sampling of cells where it is expected that a large number of the cells are actively reproducing. The very tip of a growing onion root is one such location.

Tearing a green onion from the soil where it is growing will often rip away all the fine root tips. The best way to harvest an onion is to lift up the soil around the onion bulb and then gently wash away the soil to reveal the complete root structure. Keeping the bottom of the root bulb in water will encourage the root tips to keep growing until it is time to make observations.

Using a sharp razor blade, cut the very tip of one root away. Place the tip on a microscope slide, add one drop of water with an eyedropper, and cover with a cover glass. Place a tissue over the cover glass and apply gentle pressure. Apply enough pressure to flatten the tip slightly without breaking the fragile cover slip. Introduce one drop of iodine stain to one edge of the cover glass and watch as the iodine moves across and reaches the onion root tip. Touching the edge of the cover slip on the side opposite the iodine with a torn piece of tissue will cause some of the water to be wicked up by the tissue, and the iodine will be drawn over to where the onion root tip is located.

Observe the onion cells under low and then medium power. Switch to high power and gently move the slide until cells can be found that are undergoing mitosis. Make drawings of these observations, and attempt to label cell parts.

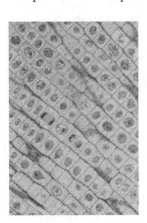

Onion root tip cells

9.1.2.1d - *select and integrate information from various sources, including electronic and print resources, community resources, and personally collected data, to answer the questions chosen*

INFORMATION FROM VARIOUS SOURCES

Cloning is a controversial issue that has scientists all around the world debating the pros and cons. To fully understand issues like this, students should also fully understand the science behind them and why it causes problems for some people. When investigating issues, it is more important than ever to research the issue using various sources.

Using a number of resources will hopefully present the student with new ideas and provide food for thought. A balanced argument can then be made that takes into consideration all sides of an issue.

9.1.2.1e - *organize, record, and analyse the information gathered*

9.1.2.1f - *predict the value of a variable by interpolating or extrapolating from graphical data*

PREDICT

An important skill to develop is the ability to predict the value of a variable by extrapolating or interpolating from graphical data. **Extrapolation** is the process of identifying new data points outside a particular set of known data points. It is similar to the process of **interpolation**, which identifies new points between known points.

For example, analyze the graphic representation entitled **Reproductive Performance** and try to predict trends for upcoming years. If you were to actually plot your prediction points as a continuation of this graph, you would have **extrapolated** data. If for some reason you needed to identify a particular value within the information provided on the graph, you would be **interpolating** data. For example, to answer the question *"At what age is a woman's likelihood of getting pregnant 70%?"*, you would need to interpolate data.

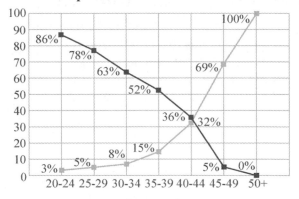

Reproductive Performance

Both of the line graphs are for women with normal reproductive function, after having unprotected intercourse for one year.

You might also gather other information, such as the **factors affecting reproductive performance** noted below, and then further predict trends or patterns of performance in upcoming years.

FACTORS AFFECTING REPRODUCTIVE PERFORMANCE

Age of the man: Although sperm remain potent even in old age, older men are more likely to experience problems with sexual function and also a decreased frequency of sexual activity.

Sexually transmitted disease: STDs are the leading cause of infertility. Chlamydia and gonorrhea cause infertility in both men and women

Nutrition: A drop below 10–15% of a woman's body weight can interfere with fertility. A woman should have at least 22% body fat to maintain regular ovulation. Eating disorders can be a major cause of infertility.

Toxins: Lead, toxic fumes, and pesticides are thought to be contributing factors for infertility in men and women.

Consider what changes or additions to this graph would look like if you predicted trends that reflected the above factors. Consider the effects of people choosing to ignore the risk factors that could be controlled—what would the consequences be and how would the results look on the graph? Conversely, what changes could be represented graphically if people make healthy choices to optimize their reproductive performance?

Graphs are very useful tools for representing patterns and trends in data. Relationships between variables can be seen and predicted.
Extrapolating and **interpolating** are techniques used to help interpret graphic material.

9.1.2.1g - *communicate scientific ideas, procedures, results, and conclusions using appropriate language and formats*

9.1.2.1h - *defend orally a position on the concern or problem investigated*

COMMUNICATE/DEFEND

Scientific language has been developed to accurately describe structures, processes, and concepts in science. People who work in science are expected to develop skills in using this language so that they can communicate more effectively with others. The language used may change depending on the audience and on whether they will be reading or listening to the information. When scientists are talking to other scientists, they may use lots of terms and jargon. If a scientist is talking to a member of the general public, he or she will be expected to provide more basic explanations and perhaps include examples or analogies to make things easier to understand. Jargon is the collection of terminology or words and phrases that relate to a specific activity, profession, or group. It is usually developed in order for that group to communicate more quickly and effectively. For example, doctors and medical professionals may communicate this way when they need to communicate quickly and effectively, like while performing surgery or dealing with an emergency situation. Another common place for jargon is in e-mail. As you know, there are many commonly used expressions that are used simply for the sake of quickness. "LOL" is commonly understood to mean laughing out loud, and "POS" means parent over shoulder! Another feature of jargon is that often only the people belonging to the group using it, understand it. To use jargon with a group who does not understand it, would be inappropriate for a scientist trying to convey information.

Data should be presented in an organized fashion. To communicate trends or relationships in data, visual representations are often used to make the data more meaningful. For example, if a teacher surveyed her class to find out what kind of ice cream was preferred by students, she might record the students' answers on the dry erase board in the classroom using quick headings. This collection of data would be considered *raw data*. Raw data is simply data in its unprocessed form.

Favourite Types of Ice Cream for Class 9B

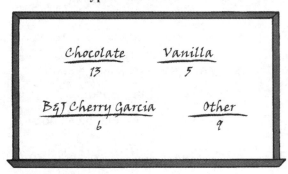

In order to communicate this collected data most clearly and effectively, the teacher would translate the raw data into some sort of organized table or chart. Data presented this way would also be effective as an aid when explaining or defending a scientific question because it presents meaningful data in a way that is easily and quickly understood.

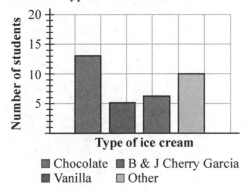

Favourite Types of Ice Cream for Class 9B

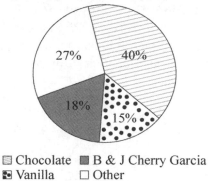

Different ways of organizing data highlight different things. Choice of presentation and language may differ depending on the audience and the information being communicated.

9.1.2.2 *use a microscope to observe and identify (in living tissue and prepared slides) animal and vegetable cells in different stages of mitosis, as well as cells undergoing asexual reproduction*

EXAMINING CELLS WITH MICROSCOPES

Living organisms reproduce in a number of ways. One of the most simple forms of reproduction is called mitosis. Mitosis is the process in which a cell with a nucleus separates into two identical daughter cells. Every nucleus contains genetic material in bundled coils called DNA. These bundles are formed from gathered chromosomes. During mitosis, the chromosomes separate into two identical sets, in two daughter nuclei, within the parent cell's nucleus. The parent cell divides in two. The result is the formation of two identical daughter cells, each with identical genetic material. Plant and animal cells both have a nucleus, though the way the parent cells divide is somewhat different for each. The animal cell membrane cleaves and pinches off in the middle to produce two cells, whereas the plant cell forms into two separate cells as a result of the daughter cells building a new cell wall that separates the original parent cell.

Examine the diagram of animal cell mitosis and identify where there would be differences in plant cell division. Could you draw the phases of mitosis for a plant cell? You might use a reference book or the Internet to help you gather information.

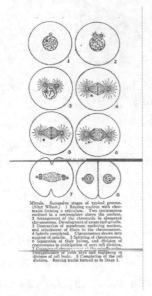

Animal cell mitosis

Budding is another form of reproduction where new individuals form from outgrowths (buds) on the bodies of mature organisms. These outgrowths develop by means of mitotic cell division. Some unicellular organisms, such as yeast, reproduce this way. Some plants, fungi, and even simple animals also reproduce this way. The offspring are exact clones of the parent.

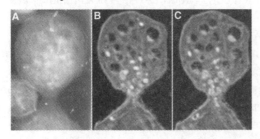

Yeast cell budding

If you looked at examples of mitosis in plant and animal cells, as well as budding in yeast cells under a microscope, what features might you notice that would help you to differentiate between the different processes?

Use the following information to answer the next question.

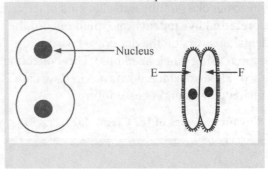

20. Which of the following types of asexual reproduction is depicted in the diagram?

   A. Fission   **B.** Budding

   C. Regeneration   **D.** Fragmentation

9.1.2.3 *design and conduct an investigation into the stages of cell division to determine changes taking place in the nucleus and cell membrane*

INVESTIGATIONS IN CELL DIVISION

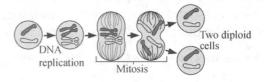

Major events in mitosis

The demonstration described below is one way a group of students could better understand what major changes take place in the cell membrane and nucleus during mitosis, or cell division.

HUMAN MITOSIS DEMONSTRATION

Students act the parts of the major players in mitosis. In this model, students form a large circle representing the cell membrane.

Inside the cell membrane, two girls represent sister chromatids of a maternal chromosome. Two boys represent the sister chromatids of the paternal chromosome. Each of these homologous pairs (the maternal and the paternal) link arms. This represents the centromere for each pair. Another group of students form a nuclear membrane around the chromosomes.

Two students stand outside the nucleus to represent the centrioles that will migrate to the poles. These students can hold twine to represent spindle fibres.

Now imagine that the Teacher calls out the phases of mitosis, students enact the events.

Prophase—nuclear membrane "breaks down" (students disperse into the "cytoplasm" of the cell). In a real cell, the chromosomes would become visible, but in the model the students cannot exactly be invisible and then appear—Oh the limitations of models!

Metaphase—chromosomes line up along the equator (middle of "cell"), centrioles migrate to poles (front & back of the "cell").

Anaphase—spindle fibres attach to centromeres (students have to use hands for this part), begin to pull chromatids toward poles.

Telophase—nuclear membranes re-form around the chromosomes at each pole, forming two new nuclei. Each nucleus now contains an unduplicated paternal chromosome and an unduplicated maternal chromosome.

Repeat. Try to make it a smooth uninterrupted process, fluid. It is a nice reinforcement of the concepts. Have students as much as possible plan the activity. Plan ahead and have students wear colour–coded clothing for an even more dramatic effect. A nice open space obviously helps.

9.1.3.1 *describe the use of reproductive technologies in a workplace environment and explain the costs and benefits of using such technologies*

9.1.3.4 *provide examples of the impact of developments in reproductive biology on global and local food production, populations, the spread of disease, and the environment*

IMPACT OF TECHNOLOGY

There have been many developments in the area of reproductive biology in recent years. These developments impact local and global food production, populations, the spread of disease, and the environment. Some developments are seen as helpful, others are seen as negative, but most are seen as having both positive and negative effects. Still others are inconclusive because more time is needed to determine whether the effects are positive or negative. What seems like a great improvement initially, could ultimately turn out to create a new set of problems. There are many examples of developments in reproductive biology that have had an impact on everyday life. For example, the genetic engineering of crops, reproductive technologies that assist organisms, including humans, in the process of becoming pregnant, and the production of hybrid species.

Reproductive technologies for humans have been developed relatively recently in order to assist the natural process of fertilization and impregnation. The issues surrounding this area are at times very sensitive and ethical in nature. These technologies have enabled people to conceive who for some reason were not able to do so naturally in a reasonable time period. As you can imagine, this has brought great joy to some families. For others, the employed techniques are unsuccessful, causing even further disappointment. There is some research suggesting that fertilization achieved through some types of assisted means may increase the risk for birth defects. There is also research that indicates that the likelihood of multiple births increases when assisted reproductive techniques are used.

Another example from the area of reproductive biology is in the genetic modification or engineering of commercial crops. The goal of this is generally to produce a greater yield. Well over 80% of the canola grown in Canada is genetically modified. The edible oil extracted from the plants is generally seen as one of the most healthy table oils in the world. It is grown all over the world but was developed in Canada. The genetically modified plants are very hardy and resistant to insect pests. Some scientists have concerns that a genetically modified food may not be healthy for humans to consume in the long term. There is also some concern that organically grown or simply non-genetically modified crops are becoming harder and harder to grow because they are being contaminated by adjacent genetically modified crops. Natural strains are becoming more difficult to protect, and may prove to be very important down the road.

Canola field near Red Deer, Alberta

A process called hybridization is used in farming or animal husbandry operations. Hybrid organisms are a combination of more than one variety or even species. In plant and animal breeding, hybrids are commonly produced and selected because they have desirable characteristics not found or inconsistently present in the parent individuals or populations. When two organisms mate or are bred, their genetic material is combined. There are many cases in which this happens naturally and there are cases in which humans facilitate the process. The main drawback of hybridization is that genetic diversity is decreased. Biodiversity is very important in maintaining healthy and viable ecosystems and populations. For example, if plants that have been hybridized for the purposes of agriculture spread to the wild, they will affect the wild gene pool. Usually, the naturally occurring organisms have traits that are better suited to withstanding the pressures of their natural environment. If the wild population is weakened by the spillover that can occur, it may jeopardize the future viability of that population.

Zorse

The field of reproductive technology is very interesting and has many different areas to explore and learn about. It is important to think about why humans want to explore this area and to consider the ethical issues that surround many of these areas of scientific research and development. The consequences of artificially manipulating genetic material are significant. There are benefits and drawbacks that must be carefully considered. The consequences for the long term are difficult to anticipate and must be carefully considered from an ethical and biological perspective.

Use the following information to answer the next question.

> Farmers often select plants that have certain advantages, such as resistance to pests, and use their seeds to grow better crops. This is known as selective breeding. However, extensive selective breeding can lead to major disadvantages.

21. Which of the following results is a disadvantage of extensive selective breeding?

   A. Alteration of genes

   B. Loss of biodiversity

   C. Loss of natural minerals

   D. Disturbance in the ecological cycle

9.1.3.2 *examine some Canadian contributions to research and technological development in the field of genetics and reproductive biology*

CANADIAN CONTRIBUTIONS TO RESEARCH AND TECHNOLOGICAL DEVELOPMENT IN THE FIELD OF GENETICS AND REPRODUCTIVE BIOLOGY

Researchers and scientists worldwide contribute to the collective knowledge base. When a cure for a disease or improved farming technique is discovered or developed, that knowledge usually becomes available to others. It benefits people in other parts of the world. Among other areas, Canadian scientists and researchers have contributed to the body of research and technological development in the field of genetics and reproductive biology.

Seeds and cells of organisms contain genetic information. This information directs all activities of living things, including growth, development and reproduction. Genetic material can be altered or artificially combined by scientists trained in genetics. Otherwise, genetic code changes gradually over time through the process of evolution, or adaptation to the environment.

The popular McIntosh apple variety was originally cultivated by a Canadian named John McIntosh. Every McIntosh apple has a direct genetic link (lineage) to a single tree discovered in 1811 by this particular farmer in Ontario.

McIntosh apple.

The McIntosh apple is an apple cultivar. A **cultivar** is a cultivated plant that has been selected and given a unique name because of its decorative or useful characteristics; it is usually distinct from similar plants and when propagated it retains those characteristics. Put simply, cultivars can be grown over and over again and will be very similar every time. They may occur naturally or may have been combined artificially by human manipulation.

Copyright Protected

Another example of a very successful cultivar used for agricultural purposes is canola. Canola is a type of edible oil used worldwide. It was initially bred in Canada in the 1970's. The word canola comes from "**Can**adian **oi**l, **l**ow **a**cid" which represents a description of the oil produced by this variety of rapeseed.

Canola field in Alberta.

Canadians have made other contributions to research and technological development in the field of reproductive biology and genetics. In 1989, a team of researchers at the Hospital for Sick Children in Toronto discovered the gene responsible for Cystic Fibrosis, a hereditary disease that's onset begins in infancy or early childhood. This disease affects the mucus glands of the lungs, liver, pancreas, and intestines. People affected by this disease may have frequent lung infections, poor growth, and a much shorter than normal life expectancy. The discovery of this gene is helpful in learning more about the disease. It has already led to improvements in care of people affected by CF, and may eventually contribute to the development of a cure.

Canadian scientists and researchers have made many contributions to the field of reproductive biology. Their contributions make a real difference in some way, whether it is economic, medical, or research development-based.

Practice

22. A major Canadian contribution to the field of genetics has been a genetically modified crop used to produced a healthy oil called
   A. sesame seed oil   **B.** vegetable oil
   C. canola oil   **D.** olive oil

9.1.3.3 *identify local environmental factors and individual choices that may lead to a change in a cell's genetic information or an organism's development, and investigate the consequences such factors and choices have on human development*

FACTORS IN CELL DEVELOPMENT

People are exposed to many substances and chemicals in their everyday lives. These substances or chemicals are called environmental factors. Environmental factors differ depending on where a person spends their time. There are airborne substances everywhere. For example, in or near cities, the emissions from vehicles, factories, and industrial plants may be many. Cigarette smoke may be almost unavoidable. There are substances taken in through food and water that are virtually unavoidable. There are other things, such as medical X-rays, that can cause cell damage or alteration if done under certain circumstances or with a certain intensity or amount. Some of the substances people are exposed to can alter cells or change normal growth patterns. Generally, healthy people can carry on feeling unaffected by the exposure to toxins. Some exposure is simply unavoidable, but there are choices people make that can increase or reduce their exposure to potentially harmful chemicals.

Class Focus   34   Castle Rock Research

The first exposure to potential toxins occurs when a fetus is growing inside its mother's uterus. Though research shows that the benefits of breastfeeding outweigh the drawbacks, toxins that have accumulated in a woman's tissues will be transmitted to her baby through breast milk. Research shows that the younger a child is when he or she is exposed to harmful substances, the more susceptible that child is to being harmed. This includes developing fetuses. Developing babies who are exposed to cigarette smoke, whether first- or second-hand, have been shown to have lower birth weights than babies who have not been exposed to cigarette smoke. Children who live in homes where they are continually exposed to smoke tend to have an increased likelihood of coughing, wheezing, sore throats, respiratory problems, and potentially even asthma. Removing the exposure can greatly improve any negative effects that have been seen. Chemicals or environmental factors that cause birth defects are called teratogens. These types of birth defects may be preventable in some cases.

People routinely receive medical X-rays for things like monitoring dental health or to have injuries diagnosed. The strength of the radiation transmitted for medical X-rays differs for different types of X-rays, and cells can be altered or normal growth patterns changed by exposure to radiation. Fetuses are more susceptible than adults to the damaging effects of X-rays, partly because their cells are rapidly dividing and growing into specialized cells and tissues. If X-rays cause changes in these cells, there is a slightly increased chance of birth defects or certain illnesses, such as leukemia, later in life. Damage to fetal cells may also result in miscarriage, birth defects, or mental impairment, depending on the amount of radiation and the stage of pregnancy. Similarly, with the use of some prescription, and particularly non-prescription drugs, cells and growth patterns may be altered in a way that can cause a variety of damaging effects to humans.

Environmental factors and individual choices may lead to a change in a cell's genetic information or an organism's development. Human development is affected by these factors. Some are virtually unavoidable, whereas others are almost entirely avoidable by choice.

Practice

Use the following information to answer the next question.

The placenta is the embryo's life support system. Useful and harmful substances are exchanged between the mother and the fetus through the placenta, a flattened circular disc, that fits closely into the wall of the uterus.

23. Which of the following substances can be a harmful when exchanged between the mother and the developing fetus through the placenta?

A. Drugs

B. Hormones

C. Antibodies

D. Excretory products

CHALLENGER QUESTION

24. A negative effect of using chemical pesticides on the same field over a long period of time is that the

A. genetic makeup of the insects may be altered

B. chemical buildup may alter the water table level

C. insects may develop a resistance to the chemicals

D. chemicals may leach into the soil and reduce productivity

25. Which of the following issues is a concern that scientists have about the use of genetically modified crops?

   A. They are too costly for people to continue growing over the long term.

   B. They may become invasive species and spread out of control.

   C. They do not produce the same taste as the original crops.

   D. They may be harmful to people over the long term.

26. The **main** drawback in using hybridized species of plants or animals is that

   A. the cost of producing them is too high

   B. they usually fail to grow or live

   C. genetic diversity is decreased

   D. they are unable to reproduce

9.1.3.5 *describe careers that involve some aspect of reproductive biology*

CAREERS IN REPRODUCTIVE BIOLOGY

The field of reproductive biology includes a wide variety of work that is accomplished by many different types of trained professionals and technologists. This area includes anything that may pertain to reproduction. For example, there are many research scientists studying the science of reproduction. Basic research is conducted over the long term simply to keep track of data and to note trends or changes in a field such as reproductive biology.

In relatively recent years, the area of assisted reproductive technology has become an important area of scientific research in human biology. Assisted reproductive technology is a general term referring to methods used to achieve pregnancy by artificial or partially artificial means. Currently, the technology available allows various medical and technically trained individuals to assist people in achieving pregnancy. Some of these people may be laboratory researchers or technicians, ultrasound technicians, fertility counsellors, various types of doctors who specialize in the area of reproductive biology and/or fertility, surgeons, or psychologists. The role each person plays depends on the type of training they have. For example, a general practitioner, or family physician, may be the first person to find out a woman is having a difficult time becoming pregnant. The general practitioner may have various suggestions to offer or may refer the woman to a fertility specialist. A laboratory technician might be the person who actually handles or manipulates the gametes, or sex cells, involved in a situation, whereas an ultrasound technician would have the job of recording information through the use of ultrasounds images to determine what is going on inside a woman's or a man's body that may provide information that will help the doctors determine what is happening. Alternative complimentary medicine, such as acupuncture and hypnosis, is also sometimes used with humans requiring some kind of fertility counselling or intervention.

There are other types of biologists who study reproductive issues pertaining to non-human organisms. Other issues, such as cloning, population control, hybrid development, and disease resistance, are studied, and the results sometimes employed by farmers or land managers of various types.

There are a wide range of careers pertaining to reproductive biology. Some of these careers have to do with humans, while others focus on other organisms that reproduce, such as plants or animals. Various levels of training are required to become certified in any of these areas. Technicians may require one or two years of formal training to perform their jobs, while certain medical specialists require many years of education and training in order to become certified in their fields.

Practice

Use the following information to answer the next question.

A section of a bacteria's DNA is inserted into a tomato plant's DNA to prevent the tomato plant from destruction by a certain beetle.

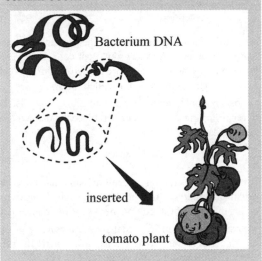

Bacterium DNA

inserted

tomato plant

27. The science that deals with the practice of using living things to alter genetic makeup is referred to as

  A. biology   **B.** biodynamics

  C. biochemistry   **D.** biotechnology

SOLUTIONS—BIOLOGY: REPRODUCTION - PROCESSES AND APPLICATIONS

1. Part A- **OR**	6. **D**	12. **D**	18. **OR**	24. **C**
Part B- **OR**	7. **B**	13. **B**	19. **B**	25. **D**
2. **C**	8. **A**	14. **D**	20. **A**	26. **C**
3. **C**	9. **C**	15. **OR**	21. **B**	27. **D**
4. **A**	10. **OR**	16. **C**	22. **C**	
5. **C**	11. **B**	17. **B**	23. **A**	

1. Part A – Open Response

Points	Sample Answer
2	One mark for each answer.
	Mitosis is cell division where two new genetically identical cells are produced.
	Meiosis is cell division where reproductive cells are produced. They contain half the genetic information of the parent cell.

Part B – Open Response

Points	Sample Answer
4	One mark each.
	• Growth of a new individual (from one cell to a baby)
	• Growth of a child (from a baby to an adult)
	• Repair of damaged tissues after an accident.
	• Replacement of cells from tissues that do not live forever (e.g., skin cells, blood cells, stomach lining).

2. C

Instead of a complete chromosome, chromatids are present at the poles of the cell. This stage is indicative of anaphase II.

In anaphase I, chromosomes are visible, and the homologous chromosomes move to the poles of the cell. In telophase I, chromosomes uncoil, and the nucleolus and nuclear membrane begin to appear. Telophase II is similar to telophase I. The chromatids begin to uncoil, and the nucleolus and nuclear membrane begin to appear.

3. C

During interphase, the cell prepares itself for division by producing protein and cytoplasmic organelles. This process takes place in three phases.

The cell grows in the first phase. In the second phase, the cell continues its growth. The synthesis and replication of DNA also take place during this phase. In the third phase, the cell prepares for division by mitosis.

The sister chromatids of each chromosome are separated during anaphase, not interphase. Chromatin condenses during prophase, not interphase. The nuclear membrane breaks down during metaphase, not interphase.

4. A

As multi-celled organisms grow, their bodies constantly undergo changes. As you grow, your cells do not grow large, but instead become more numerous through cell division. This cell division is called mitosis.

Mitosis not only helps an organism grow, but it also helps to repair injuries. Healthy cells replace the damaged cells, healing damaged tissues.

5. C

Binary fission is the type of cell division that a one-celled organism undergoes to reproduce asexually. The two new cells both have a full complement of genetic information.

Mitosis is the scientific word that describes any type of cell division where the two new cells have exactly the same genetic information as the parent cell.

Budding is a type of cell division whereby a small piece of a cell buds off to make a new cell. The new cell has the same genetic information as the parent cell.

Meiosis is the type of cell division that produces sex cells. During this process, the genetic information is split, and the two new cells have half the genetic information of the parent cells. Alternative C is the correct choice.

6. D

The DNA in cells is located in the nucleus of the cell.

7. B

The reason the nucleus can control the various cell activities is that it contains the genetic information in the form of DNA.

8. A

The diagram depicts the process of budding in a hydra. During budding, a daughter organism is formed from a small projection called the bud, which arises from the parent body. Eventually, the bud splits away from the parent and becomes a separate organism.

Syngamy is the complete and permanent fusion of male and female gametes in order to form a zygote. Parthenogenesis is the formation of an embryo directly from an egg without the fertilization of a sperm. Neurogenesis is the formation of a neural tube during embryonic development. The neural tube eventually becomes the brain, the spinal cord, and the different sensory organs.

9. C

Budding (A) is a mode of asexual reproduction in which a new individual develops from a specialized part or bud of the parent individual. Binary fission (B) is the division of the body of an individual into equal halves, each of which functions as an independent daughter individual. Fragmentation (C) is a mode of asexual reproduction in which the body of an individual breaks up into distinct pieces, each of which grows into a complete individual. In multiple fission (D), a number of daughter cells are produced from a single parent.

10. Open Response

Budding is a type of asexual reproduction in which one or more units, or multicellular buds, are formed on the parent body. Each bud consists of a small group of cells surrounded by an epithelium. A bud may become separated from the parent body and then develop into a new flower or leaf, or it may separate only after the completion of development.

11. B

There are basically two types of sexual reproduction: syngamy and conjugation. Syngamy is the complete and permanent fusion of male and female gametes in order to form the zygote. Conjugation involves the temporary union of two parents of the same species in order to exchange the male pronuclei. Fragmentation and plasmotomy are types of asexual reproduction.

12. D

Internal fertilization occurs in mammals, and a moose is a mammal. Internal fertilization is a process that takes place inside the female reproductive system.

13. B

Asexual reproduction involves one parent and does not involve fertilization.

Sexual reproduction involves two parents and involves the fertilization of male and female reproductive cells.

In order for the process of fertilization to occur, the environment must be wet. Asexual reproduction can occur in dryer environments, but it usually requires some moisture.

14. D

Sexual reproduction leads to the mixing of genetic material from two parents. This leads to genetically different offspring. Hence, the main advantage of sexual reproduction is that it leads to offspring that are genetically different from the parents.

Distractor Rationale

Sexual reproduction does not reduce the chromosome count of the offspring, it does not require two parents, and it takes more time than asexual reproduction.

15. Open Response

The main disadvantages of asexual reproduction are
- a negative mutation during DNA replication can wipe out a colony of cells
- lowered ability to cope with new diseases and environmental conditions
- vulnerability to predators for which they have no defence

16. C

The zygote is formed after fertilization. The first week after fertilization, the zygote undergoes cell division to form a ball of cells in morula formation. By the end of the week, the cells have begun to specialize in the blastula stage. Following embryonic development is the fetal stage.

17. B

The correct order of embryonic development is
fertilization → zygote → morula → blastula.

18. Open Response

Once an egg is fertilized, it is called a zygote. The first week after fertilization, the zygote undergoes cell division to form a simple ball of cells called a morula. By the end of the second week, these cells have begun to specialize. This is called the blastula stage.

19. B

Cultivation of one type of crop for many years decreases the diversity of the flora. Diversity of species is necessary to maintain a balanced ecosystem. Over many years, monoculture will tend to decrease crop production and decrease soil fertility, but it is not likely to have a strong effect on the amount of soil fauna.

The correct answer is B.

20. A

Fission is the type of asexual reproduction shown in the diagram. It is observed in unicellular organisms such as amoebas. In the process of fission, the parent organism gives rise to two daughter cells. For this reason, it is also called binary fission. Nuclear division takes place first. It is then followed by constriction of the cell membrane, which divides the cytoplasm into two parts.

Budding is a type of asexual reproduction seen in multicellular organisms such as the hydra and unicellular organisms such as yeast. Regeneration is the ability of an organism to replace its lost body parts. It also helps in the multiplication of an organism. Fragmentation involves the breaking down of an organism into two or more parts, each of which grows to form a new organism. Ribbon worms and starfish undergo fragmentation.

21. **B**

If selective breeding continues for too long, only certain varieties of crops will be grown. Other varieties that are not commercially beneficial may begin to disappear. Thus, there can be a loss of biodiversity in that particular ecosystem.

22. **C**

Well over 80% of the canola grown in Canada is genetically modified. The edible oil extracted from the plants is generally seen as one of the most healthy table oils in the world. It is grown all over the world but was developed in Canada. The genetically modified plants are very hardy and resistant to insect pests.

23. **A**

Many drugs can harm a growing fetus. The fetus is most sensitive to damage by drugs during the phase of organ development, which starts in the third week of pregnancy. All addictive drugs, such as heroin, are very dangerous to an unborn child. The baby may become addicted to them before it is born and suffer withdrawal symptoms after birth. Permanent brain damage to the fetus may occur during pregnancy, resulting in mental retardation or behavioural problems later in life.

24. **C**

A negative effect of using chemical pesticides is that insects may develop a resistance to the chemicals being used.

25. **D**

Scientists have raised concerns that the consumption of genetically modified crops may be harmful to humans in the long term.

26. **C**

The main drawback in using hybridized species is that the genetic diversity is decreased. Biodiversity is very important in maintaining healthy and viable ecosystems and populations.

27. **D**

The science that deals with the practice of using living things to alter genetic makeup is referred to as biotechnology. Biotechnology can be used to protect crops against harmful insects and increase yields in harvesting.

1. During mitosis, the parent cell produces two daughter cells containing

A. half the number of chromosomes as the parent cell

B. the same number of chromosomes as the parent cell

C. triple the number of chromosomes as the parent cell

D. double the number of chromosomes as the parent cell

Use the following information to answer the next question.

The following chart contains a list of different types of cell division in the human body.

Number	Description of Cell Division
1	Cells divide to form new egg cells.
2	Cells divide to form new skin cells.
3	Cells divide to form new bone cells.
4	Cells divide to form new sperm cells.

2. Which descriptions are examples of the type of cell division called meiosis?

A. 1 and 2   B. 1 and 4

C. 2 and 3   D. 2 and 4

Open Response

3. Sometimes, DNA may not be properly replicated during cell division. How would this cause mutations or cancer?

_____
_____
_____
_____
_____

4. Which of the following cell organelles stores genetic material?

A. Mitochondria   B. Golgi body

C. Vacuole   D. Nucleus

Use the following information to answer the next question.

A one-celled organism reproduces through the stages shown in the given illustration.

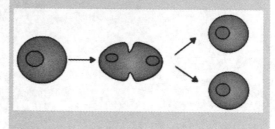

5. Which type of asexual reproduction is represented in the given illustration?

A. Fission   B. Cutting

C. Budding   D. Spore formation

6. Which of the following organisms reproduces both sexually and asexually?

A. Frog   B. Aphid

C. Euglena   D. Amoeba

Open Response

7. Describe how external fertilization works. Give two examples of species that use this method of reproduction.

_____
_____
_____
_____
_____

Use the following information to answer the next question.

The given table describes the two methods of plant reproduction.

Method X	Method Y
Pollen from neighbouring plant is brought to a flower by a bumblebee. The pollen travels down a pollen tube in the flower and fuses with an ovule. A seed is formed, and it becomes a new plant.	A stem from a plant is broken off by an animal and ends up stuck in the ground. The broken end of the stem begins to form roots, and the broken stem develops into a new plant.

8. Which of the following tables correctly identifies the methods described above?

A.

Method	Type of Reproduction
X	Budding
Y	Sexual

B.

Method	Type of Reproduction
X	Asexual
Y	Sexual

C.

Method	Type of Reproduction
X	Sexual
Y	Asexual

D.

Method	Type of Reproduction
X	Asexual
Y	Budding

9. What is the first structure formed by the initial cell division of the fertilized egg?

   A. Fetus
   B. Morula
   C. Blastula
   D. Gastrocoel

Use the following information to answer the next question.

There are several microscopes available for use when studying different types of slides. The total magnification of these microscopes depends on the magnification of the lenses used.

10. Jill views a sample under a microscope with a $10x$ eyepiece. If she uses the $50x$ objective lens, at what magnification does Jill see her sample?

   A. $4x$
   B. $40x$
   C. $400x$
   D. $4\,000x$

Use the following information to answer the next question.

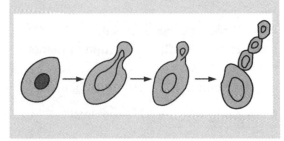

11. The method of reproduction shown in the given diagram is called

   A. cutting
   B. budding
   C. binary fission
   D. multiple fission

12. A farmer decides to use genetically engineered crops that are resistant to the pests that usually cause problems. What is the **main** advantage of using genetically modified or engineered crops?

   A. It reduces the amount of fertilizer needed.
   B. It helps kill off all natural pests for crops.
   C. A greater yield of crops is available for harvest.
   D. Crops can be made to grow in any environment.

Use the following information to answer the next question.

Scientists continue to do research in the area of reproductive technology. One such technology involves removing the reproductive cells from both the male (sperm) and female (egg) and fertilizing them in a lab before placing the zygote in a female's reproductive system.

13. What is the name of the technique described?

   A. Artificial insemination

   B. Genetic engineering

   C. In vitro fertilization

   D. Biotechnology

14. A person with a career that deals specifically with the cultivation of plants would be called a

   A. horticulturist   **B.** phylogenist

   C. ecologist   **D.** botanist

Open Response

Use the following information to answer the next question.

Zebra mussels are thought to have been brought to the Great Lakes inside the tanks of boats and cargo ships. In this new environment, they had no natural predators, so they were able to reproduce and thrive.

15. How has the resiliency of the zebra mussels affected the diversity of the Great Lakes?

_____

_____

_____

_____

_____

_____

_____

_____

SOLUTIONS

1. B	5. A	9. B	13. C
2. B	6. B	10. C	14. A
3. OR	7. OR	11. B	15. OR
4. D	8. B	12. C	

1. B

Mitosis is the division of a parent cell into two identical daughter cells, each of which has a nucleus with the same amount of DNA, the same number and type of chromosomes, and the same hereditary instructions as the parent cell. This type of division is called equational division.

2. B

Mitosis is the type of cell division whereby the two newly formed cells have the identical type and amount of genetic information as the parent cell. This type of cell division is used for growth and for repair of tissues.

Meiosis is the type of cell division in which the amount of genetic information is split between two cells. This occurs during the formation of reproductive cells.

Descriptions 1 and 4 in the table describe the formation of sex cells. Therefore, the process is meiosis. The correct answer is B.

Descriptions 2 and 4 describe cells dividing for growth (mitosis).

3. Open Response

When DNA is not properly replicated, which sometimes happens, cell division can become uncontrolled, resulting in mutations. Both the growth and ability of a cell to reproduce can be harmed, resulting in uncontrolled cell growth, which is a type of cancer.

4. D

To answer this question correctly, the student must understand that the nucleus contains nuclear material, which consists of genetic material, such as DNA and RNA.

Distractor Rationale

A. Mitochondria produce the energy required for cell functions. Genetic material, such as DNA and RNA, is not stored in the mitochondria.

B. The Golgi body stores and packs proteins and lipids to transport outside the cell. It does not store genetic material.

C. Vacuoles perform storage functions. Their main function is to store food and secrete enzymes. They do not store genetic material.

5. A

Fission is when one cell splits into two equally sized cells. The diagram shows this type of asexual reproduction.

Budding is when small pieces break off a bigger cell to make a new organism. This occurs in yeast.

Spore formation is used by some non-flowering plants.

Cutting refers to when cuttings of plants are planted to grow new plants.

6. B

Some organisms are able to reproduce both sexually and asexually. Female aphids reproduce asexually in the summer. During the winter, a sexual generation of males and females are produced. Eggs are laid that develop into young aphids.

Frogs (A) reproduce sexually, whereas euglenas (C) and amoebae (D) reproduce asexually.

7. Open Response

External fertilization is when high numbers of male and female gametes are expelled into the environment and meet by chance. External fertilization is often used by aquatic organisms, such as salmon, sea urchins, and plants.

8. B

Sexual reproduction in plants involves the use of the flower. Pollen is the male sex cell, and it fertilizes the female ovule (or egg). This then becomes a seed that develops into a new, unique plant.

Asexual reproduction in plants is achieved through vegetative propagation. This takes place when a piece of a plant is broken off or cut off and allowed to root. The new plant is genetically identical to the original.

Budding is a form of asexual reproduction.

9. **B**

To answer this question, the student must know that the morula is formed by the rapid cell division of the fertilized egg. The first structure formed by the initial cell division of the fertilized egg is the morula.

Distractor Rationale

A. The fetus is formed by differentiation of cells during the gastrula stage. It is not the first structure formed by the initial cell division of the fertilized egg. Hence, this alternative is incorrect.

C. The blastula is formed by the arrangement of cells and the formation of a cavity in the morula. It is not the first structure formed by the initial cell division of the fertilized egg. Hence, this alternative is incorrect.

D. The gastrocoel is the fluid-filled cavity present in the gastrula. It is not the first structure formed by the initial cell division of the fertilized egg. Hence, this alternative is incorrect.

The correct answer is B.

10. **C**

To calculate the magnification of the microscope, you multiply the magnification of the two lenses.

$10 \times 40 = 400$

The total magnification is $400x$.

11. **B**

The diagram shows reproduction in yeast by the process of budding. In this process, a small, bud-like projection emerges from the yeast cell. This bud gradually grows until it detaches from the parent cell, forming a new yeast cell.

12. **C**

The main advantage to using genetically modified or engineered crops is that using them typically results in greater yields for harvest. Farmers can plant modified crops that are resistant to the pests that usually destroy crops, allowing for successful grow.

13. **C**

Artificial insemination is when the sperm of a male is taken and placed in the reproductive system of a female. This technique is often used in farming livestock.

Genetic engineering involves manipulating and changing DNA in organisms to suit specific needs.

In vitro fertilization is when an egg from a female and sperm from a male are taken and allowed to unite in a petri dish in a lab. This results in the formation of a new individual, which can be placed back inside a female reproductive system to allow for development.

Alternative C is the correct choice.

Biotechnology is any technology that is used to alter or change a biological process.

14. **A**

Horticulturalists deal specifically with the cultivation of plants. They study plant breeding and genetic engineering as well as plant biochemistry and plant physiology.

15. **Open Response**

Since the zebra mussel has no natural predators and is thriving, it has been classified as an invasive species. They have reduced the diversity of life in the Great Lakes by eating food usually eaten by other organisms that live there. This has left native organisms with less food and has led to a larger population of zebra mussels.

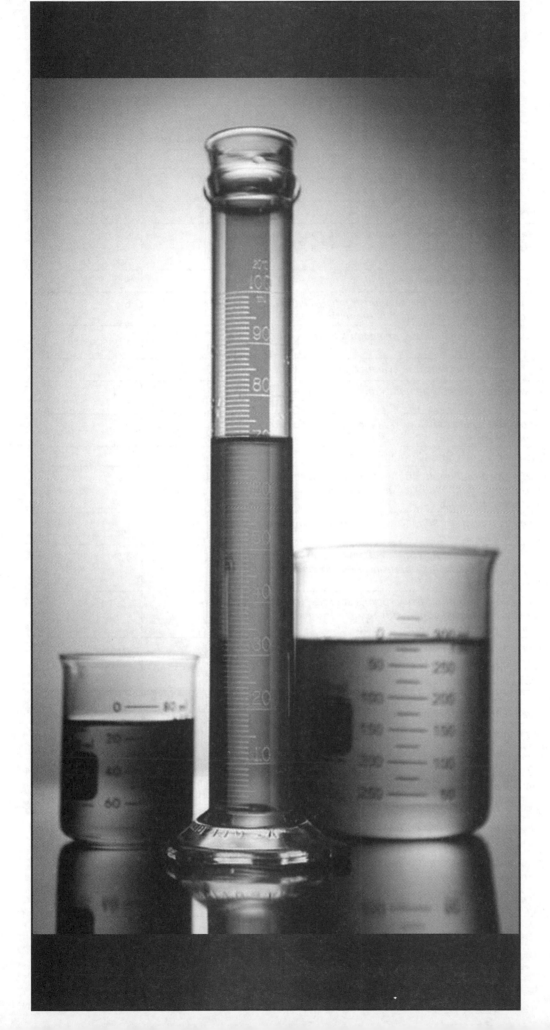

Chemistry: Exploring Matter
Table of Correlations

Specific Expectation		Practice Questions	Unit Test Questions
9.2.1	Understanding Basic Concepts		
9.2.1.1	*describe an element as a pure substance made up of one type of particle or atom with its own distinct properties*	1, 2	1
9.2.1.3	*describe compounds and elements in terms of molecules and atoms*	4, 5	3
9.2.1.4	*identify each of the three fundamental particles (neutron, proton, and electron), and its charge, location, and relative mass in a simple atomic model*	6, 7	4
9.2.1.5	*identify general features of the periodic table*	8	5
9.2.1.6	*demonstrate an understanding of the relationship between the properties of elements and their position in the periodic table*	9	6
9.2.1.7	*identify and write symbols/formulae for common elements and compounds*	10, 11	7
9.2.1.8	*describe, using their observations, the evidence for chemical changes*	12	8
9.2.1.9	*distinguish between metals and nonmetals and identify their characteristic properties*	13	9, 10
9.2.1.2	*recognize compounds as pure substances that may be broken down into elements by chemical means*	3	2
9.2.2	Developing Skills of Inquiry and Communication		
9.2.2.1a	*"through investigations and applications of basic concepts: - demonstrate knowledge of laboratory, safety, and disposal procedures while conducting investigations"*	14	11
9.2.2.1c	*- formulate scientific questions about a problem or issue involving the properties of substances*		
9.2.2.1d	*- demonstrate the skills required to plan and conduct an inquiry into the properties of substances, using apparatus and materials safely, accurately, and effectively*		13
9.2.2.1e	*- select and integrate information from various sources, including electronic and print resources, community resources, and personally collected data, to answer the questions chosen*		
9.2.2.1f	*- organize, record, and analyse the information gathered*		
9.2.2.1g	*- communicate scientific ideas, procedures, results, and conclusions using appropriate language and formats*		
9.2.2.2	*investigate, by laboratory experiment or classroom demonstration, the chemical properties of representative families of elements*	16	
9.2.2.3	*investigate the properties of changes in substances, and classify them as physical or chemical based on experiments*	17	14, 15
9.2.2.4	*construct molecular models of simple molecules*		
9.2.2.1b	*- determine how the properties of substances influence their use*	15	12
9.2.3	Relating Science to Technology, Society, and the Environment		
9.2.3.1	*identify uses of elements in everyday life*	18	16
9.2.3.3	*explain how a knowledge of the physical and chemical properties of elements enables people to determine the potential uses of the elements and assess the associated risks*	20	
9.2.3.4	*identify and describe careers that require knowledge of the physical and chemical properties of elements and compounds*	21	

	Specific Expectation	Practice Questions	Unit Test Questions
9.2.3.2	*describe the methods used to obtain elements in Canada, and outline local environmental concerns and health and safety issues related to the ways in which they are mined and processed*	19	

9.2.1.1 *describe an element as a pure substance made up of one type of particle or atom with its own distinct properties*

ELEMENTS

Matter can be defined as anything that has mass and occupies space. The book you are reading has mass and takes up space. It is made of matter. You take up space and have mass. You are made of matter. Each type of matter is made from different elements and compounds.

The flow chart below shows how matter is organized and how elements fit into the scheme of things.

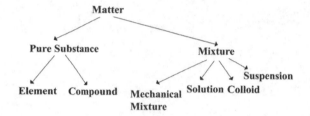

An **element** is a **pure substance** that is composed of one type of particle or atom. The element copper has only copper atoms and no other kind. Hydrogen consists only of hydrogen atoms. Copper, hydrogen, oxygen, iron, gold, and silver are common elements that most people have seen or heard of. Technetium, promethium, and seaborgium are elements that were scientifically created and very few people have heard of.

Most elements are in the solid state at room temperature. Some elements, however, do exist as a liquid or a gas at room temperature.

- Solid—gold, copper, carbon
- Liquid—mercury
- Gas—oxygen, nitrogen, argon

Scientists have identified 117 elements. Of these 117 elements, 93 are **naturally occurring** and are found somewhere on Earth. The other 24 elements have been **artificially created** in a science lab.

Each element is composed of one type of atom with distinct properties. This makes the element copper different from the element iron.

Copper	Iron
Brownish in colour	Gray in colour
Melts at 1 083°C	Melts at 1 535°C
Boils at 2 567°C	Boils at 2 750°C
Does not rust	Rusts
Conducts electricity well	Does not conduct electricity well
Has a density of 8.9 g/cm³	Has a density of 7.9 g/cm³

The five most abundant elements on Earth are

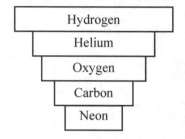

INTERESTING INFOBIT

The total number of elements present is changing. Scientific research has permitted scientists to discover new elements. Today, the number of elements that have been classified has risen to 117 from an original 93.

Practice

Use the following information to answer the next question.

An element is a homogenous substance that cannot be split by chemical means into two or more simpler substances. It cannot, therefore, be made by the chemical combination of two or more substances. An element might undergo an increase in weight, for example when S forms SO_2. This is because elements can combine with other substances, but they can never be split.

1. Which of the following statements regarding elements is **true**?

    A. Elements are made up of different types of atoms.

    B. Elements are made up of at least two types of atoms.

    C. Elements can be further subdivided into smaller particles by ordinary chemical means.

    D. Elements cannot be further subdivided into smaller particles by ordinary chemical means.

Open Response

Use the following information to answer the next question.

Matter can be defined as anything that has mass and takes up space. Each type of matter is made up of different types of elements and compounds.

2. What are elements? Provide an example of an element along with your explanation.

    _____
    _____
    _____
    _____
    _____

9.2.1.2 *recognize compounds as pure substances that may be broken down into elements by chemical means*

COMPOUNDS

Matter is all the "stuff" in the universe. This "stuff" includes pure substances made up of elements and compounds. Elements are composed of one kind of atom and cannot be broken down any further. Elements can, however, combine with other elements to form compounds.

A compound is defined as a pure substance that is composed of two or more different elements that have chemically combined with each other. Baking soda is a white powder used to make a cake rise and become fluffy. Baking soda is a molecular compound that is composed of the elements:

- Sodium (Na)
- Hydrogen (H)
- Oxygen (O)
- Carbon (C)

Sodium, hydrogen, oxygen, and carbon atoms bond together in certain proportions to form a compound that appears the same throughout. That compound is always a white powder and has certain distinct properties. The properties of baking soda are totally different from the properties of the elements that make up baking soda.

A compound can be broken down by chemical means. It might be broken down into simpler compounds, or into its elements. Water is a compound composed of hydrogen and oxygen atoms. Passing electricity through water using a process called electrolysis, causes the water molecule to break down into its elements, hydrogen and oxygen. The hydrogen and oxygen are in the form of two different gases.

Electrolysis of water

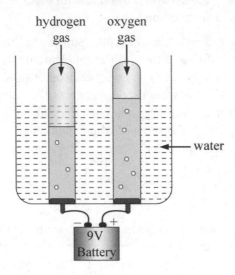

Certain compounds can be broken down into their elements by applying heat. When mercury (II) oxide, a reddish compound, is heated, it breaks down into the elements mercury and oxygen gas.

Practice

3. Sodium hydroxide is formed by the reaction of sodium oxide and water. This means that sodium hydroxide is **best** classified as

   A. a compound   B. an element

   C. a mixture   D. an atom

9.2.1.3 *describe compounds and elements in terms of molecules and atoms*

MOLECULES AND ATOMS

James was given a small piece of aluminium metal to hold in his hand. He was holding the element **aluminium** (Al). He was holding a substance that is composed of one kind of atom, and one that cannot be broken down by ordinary means.

The small piece of aluminium that James was holding consists of billions and billions of aluminium atoms. Atoms are extremely tiny particles that are the building blocks of elements.

Justine filled a teaspoon with table salt and was about to pour it into the soup she was cooking. She was about to use the compound **sodium chloride** (NaCl); a compound that is composed of two elements, **sodium** (Na) and **chlorine** (Cl).

The compound sodium chloride is composed of molecules. Molecules are made up of **atoms** of elements that are held together by chemical bonds. Table salt is made up of molecules of the sodium atom bonded to the chlorine atom in a regular pattern.

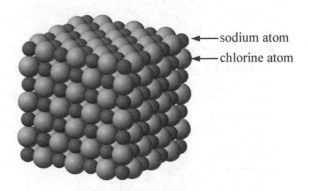
sodium atom
chlorine atom

Molecules may be composed of two or more non-identical atoms, that is, atoms from different elements. The water molecule is composed of two hydrogen atoms bonded to one oxygen atom.

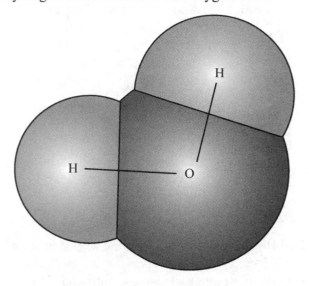

Molecules may also be composed of one or more **identical atoms**. An oxygen molecule is made from the bonding together of two identical oxygen atoms.

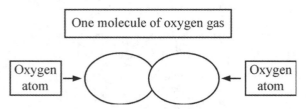

Keep in mind that a compound must be composed of two or more **different** atoms. Oxygen gas (O_2) is classified as an element molecule, not a compound molecule.

SUMMARY

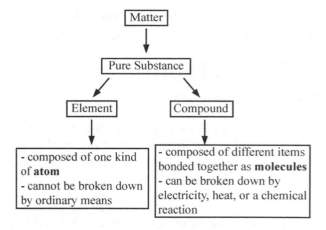

Practice

Open Response

4. How does electrolysis break down a water molecule?

_____

_____

_____

_____

Use the following information to answer the next question.

This is a picture of the atoms that make up the methane gas.

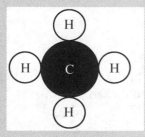

5. Why is methane considered a molecule?

   A. It is found as a gas.

   B. It can only be made in a lab.

   C. It is made up of only one type of atom.

   D. It is made up of more than one type of atom.

9.2.1.4 *identify each of the three fundamental particles (neutron, proton, and electron), and its charge, location, and relative mass in a simple atomic model*

NEUTRONS, PROTONS, AND ELECTRONS

The atom is the basic component from which all matter is made. The atom is extremely small. In fact, the size of an atom compared to an apple is like comparing an apple to the size of the Earth. That is small!

In 1981, when the Scanning Tunneling Microscope (STM) was developed, the first pictures of rows of atoms were taken. This picture shows how the sodium and chlorine atoms are arranged to form sodium chloride or table salt.

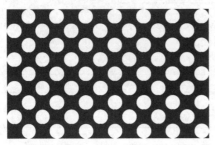

THREE FUNDAMENTAL PARTICLES OF ATOMS

Each atom has smaller subatomic particles in its structure.

• Protons
• Electrons
• Neutrons

The properties of the subatomic particles are summarized in the chart below.

Property	Proton	Electron	Neutron
Charge	Positive (+)	Negative (−)	No Charge
Location	Stationary in the nucleus	Orbiting around the nucleus	Stationary in the nucleus
Mass	Large (same size as the neutron)	Small (2 000 times smaller than the proton and neutron)	Large (same size as the proton)

Neil Bohr is credited with the first workable model of the atom. His model represents the atom as a nucleus of protons and neutrons surrounded by orbiting electrons. His model is simple to understand and is used today to explain how an atom behaves.

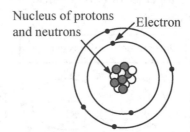

A more realistic model of the Bohr's atom shows the electrons orbiting the nucleus in a random path rather than a fixed path.

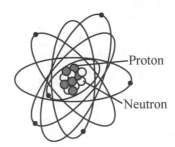

Today, scientist use the model of quantum mechanics to explain the structure of the atom. This model shows the electrons moving in a cloud, releasing energy as they move around the nucleus.

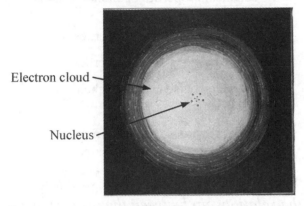

Electron cloud

Nucleus

INTERESTING INFOBIT

An easy way to remember the subatomic particles in an atom is to remember your writing utensil: PEN.
The letters in the word PEN stand for proton, electron, and neutron.

 Practice

Open Response

Use the following information to answer the next question.

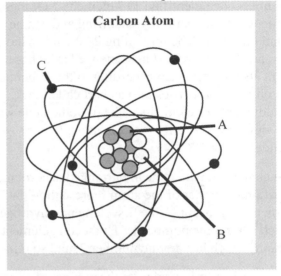

Carbon Atom

C

A

B

6. Label each part of the atom shown here (A – C) and also indicate the charge each constituent particle carries.

_____

_____

_____

_____

_____

7. Of the constituent particles of an atom
   A. only neutrons are present in the nucleus
   B. the entire negative charge is carried by electrons
   C. the major portion of the nucleus is covered by neutrons
   D. both electrons and neutrons are present inside the nucleus

9.2.1.5 *identify general features of the periodic table*

THE PERIODIC TABLE

Scientists have identified 117 elements. Of these elements, 93 are naturally occurring and can be found on Earth. The remaining 24 elements have been artificially created in a science lab. These elements are organized according to their chemical and physical properties into a chart called the periodic table of elements. The periodic table was first developed by a Russian scientist, Dmitri Mendeleev, in 1869.

The elements in the table are arranged according to the atomic number of the atom representing the element. For example, the first element is hydrogen, which has atomic number 1. The second element is helium, which has atomic number 2, and so on.

The **atomic number** refers to the number of protons in the nucleus.

- Hydrogen (atomic number 1) has 1 proton
- Helium (atomic number 2) has 2 protons
- Uranium (atomic number 92) has 92 protons

The periodic table of elements is constructed with vertical **groups** (sometimes called families) and horizontal **periods**.

- Elements located in a certain **group** have similar physical and chemical properties. There are 18 groups of elements.
- Elements located in a certain **period** have the same number of energy levels and the same electronic configuration. There are seven periods of elements.

The illustration of the periodic table shows the arrangement of **Groups** and **Periods**.

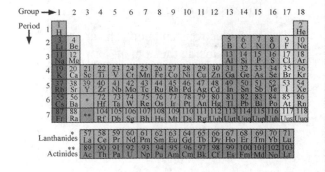

8. Which of the following statements about the chemical properties of elements in the same group is **true**?
   A. They have different properties.
   B. They have the same properties.
   C. The elements have close chemical similarities.
   D. The properties of the alternate elements are exactly the same.

9.2.1.6 *demonstrate an understanding of the relationship between the properties of elements and their position in the periodic table*

GROUPS OF THE PERIODIC TABLE

The arrangement of elements in the periodic table is based on similarities of their physical and chemical properties. Those elements that have properties of metals appear on the left side of the table, and those that have properties of nonmetals appear on the right side.

Elements with similar chemical and physical properties are placed in vertical columns called groups. Three distinct groupings of elements includes:

- Group 1—Alkali metals
- Group 17—Halogens
- Group 18—Noble gases

All alkali metals belong to Group 1 in the periodic table because they have certain properties in common. All alkali metals:

- have one electron in their outermost shell or ring
- are very reactive, particularly when in contact with water
- include the elements: lithium, sodium, potassium, cesium, and rubidium

Group 1   Alkali Metals

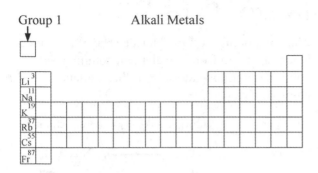

The halogen elements are located in Group 17 in the periodic table. All halogen elements

- are classified as nonmetals
- have 7 electrons in their outer ring
- tend to combine with metals to produce a form of "salt"
- includes the elements: fluorine, chlorine, bromine, iodine, and astatine

Group 17

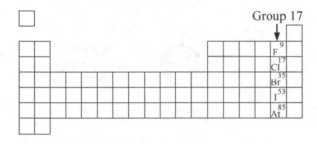

The noble gases are a small group of unique elements. All noble elements

- are in the gas state
- are inert—they do not react with other elements to form compounds
- are extremely stable because they have a complete outer ring of electrons
- include the elements: neon, argon, krypton, xenon, and radon

Noble Gases   Group 18

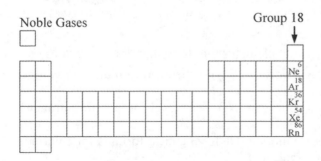

Where do the remaining groups of elements fit in? There is a slow transition from the metals to the nonmetals as one goes from the left side to the right side of the periodic table. Some elements are transitional metals, others are metalloids. Transitional metals are found in Groups 3 to 12. They have the characteristics of metals but differ in the way they combine with nonmetals to form compounds. Metalloids are at the borderline between metals and nonmetals. Metalloids are found in a diagonal line between Groups 13 and 16. Metalloids have properties of metals and nonmetals.

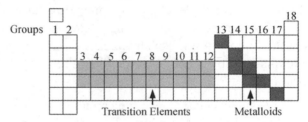

Practice

Use the following information to answer the next question.

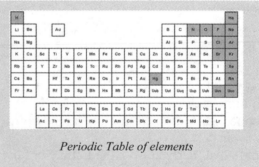

Periodic Table of elements

9. Which of the following pairs of elements in the periodic table are placed in the halogen category and the metalloid category, respectively?

   A. Cl and Mg   B. B and Ar

   C. Ne and Na   D. F and Si

9.2.1.7 *identify and write symbols/formulae for common elements and compounds*

WRITING SYMBOLS/FORMULAE FOR COMMON ELEMENTS AND COMPOUNDS

Writing out the complete word for the names of elements and compounds is a time-consuming process. It is a much simpler task to write down a letter symbol for that element. In 1813, Berzelius, a Swedish scientist, developed a simple, logical system for naming elements using a letter or letters from the Latin and English alphabets. This naming system is used by scientists throughout the world today.

Berzelius suggested that a single capital letter or a capital letter followed by a lowercase letter be used. Because Latin was the common language in Berzelius' time, many of the symbols come from the Latin root of the element.

Example

- Hydrogen—H
- Helium—He
- Oxygen—O
- Carbon—C
- Chlorine—Cl
- Copper—Cu (derived from the Latin word *cuprum*)
- Gold—Au (derived from the Latin word *aurum*)
- Sodium—Na (derived from the Latin word *natrium*)

An element is defined as matter that is composed of one kind of atom. Atoms in an element join together to form new molecular compounds. Letter symbols can be used to determine the chemical formula for these atoms and the compounds they form.

EXAMPLE

The compound sodium chloride (NaCl) is formed when one atom from the element sodium (Na) combines with one atom from the element chlorine (Cl).

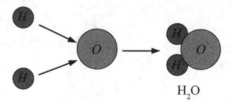

sodium + chlorine ⟶ sodium chloride

Na + Cl ⟶ Na Cl

EXAMPLE

Now consider the formula for water: H_2O
The formula shows us that two atoms of hydrogen chemically combine with one atom of oxygen.

2 hydrogen atoms + 1 oxygen atom ⟶ 1 molecule of water

H_2O

EXAMPLE

O_2 is an element because it contains only oxygen atoms. When two oxygen atoms combine together, they form a diatomic molecule ("di" means 2; "atomic" means atom).

2 oxygen atoms + 1 oxygen atom ⟶ 1 oxygen diatomic molecule

O_2

Other elements that form diatomic molecules are

- hydrogen (H_2)—chemical formula for hydrogen gas
- nitrogen (N_2)—chemical formula for nitrogen gas
- chlorine (Cl_2)—chemical formula for chlorine gas

Practice

Open Response

10. What is the chemical formula for ammonia?

_____

_____

11. What is the chemical formula of baking soda?

  A. $CaCO_3$ **B.** Na_2CO_3

  C. $NaHCO_3$ **D.** $Ca(OH)_2$

9.2.1.8 *describe, using their observations, the evidence for chemical changes*

EVIDENCE OF CHEMICAL CHANGES

When vinegar is added to baking soda, fizzing takes place. A chemical reaction occurs and the liquid vinegar and solid baking soda change into three new products, one of which is carbon dioxide gas.

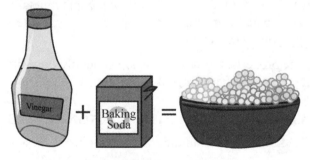

Carbon dioxide gas is formed

There are five main **indicators** that the atoms have rearranged and a chemical change has taken place.

1. Formation of a gas
2. Formation of a solid precipitate
3. Release or absorption of heat
4. Formation of an odour
5. Colour change

Example

In a controlled experiment at school, Kevin added a short piece of magnesium strip to a beaker of diluted hydrochloric acid. Kevin knew that a chemical change had occurred because

- the temperature of the liquid in the beaker rose
- bubbling and fizzing was occurring

In this chemical change:

hydrochloric acid reacts with *magnesium* to produce *magnesium chloride, hydrogen gas,* and *heat energy*

Example

Kara heated a tablespoon of sugar in butter in a saucepan for several minutes. The sugar turned brown and started to smell. A chemical change had taken place. The indicators were:

- change in colour
- release of an odour

In this chemical change:

Sugar, in the presence of *oxygen* and *heat,* changed into *carbon, carbon dioxide gas,* and *water*

Carbon is the burnt sugar.

Example

In another controlled experiment at school, Jacob added a solution of potassium iodide (clear liquid) to a solution of lead nitrate (clear liquid). He was surprised to find that a bright yellow colour resulted and a solid was formed. The evidence that a chemical reaction had taken place was:

In this experiment:

potassium iodide reacted with *lead nitrate* to produce *lead iodide* and *potassium nitrate.*

Lead iodide is the yellow precipitate.

It is important to realize that sometimes a colour change and bubbling can be a physical change rather than a chemical change.

The most common example of a chemical change is burning. When wood burns, it changes into ashes and releases a tremendous amount of heat energy.

Example

- Water added to red juice turns the juice pink
- Boiling water releases bubbles

In each of these cases, no new substances were formed. There was no rearrangement of atoms to form new molecules. Therefore, a physical change occurred.

Practice

12. Which of the following events is an example of a chemical change?
    A. Fog formation
    B. Sugar fermentation
    C. Water changing into steam
    D. Preparation of a sugar solution

9.2.1.9 *distinguish between metals and nonmetals and identify their characteristic properties*

DISTINGUISHING BETWEEN METALS AND NONMETALS

Metal elements are placed on the left side of the periodic table and nonmetal elements appear on the right side. The reason for this arrangement is that metals have different properties than nonmetals.

GENERAL PROPERTIES OF METALS

1. shiny and reflective
2. good conductors of electricity
3. good conductors of heat
4. malleable
5. ductile
6. exist as solids at room temperature (except mercury)

Copper has properties common to most metals.

Copper is a metal that has a shiny surface. This surface may eventually become dull as copper oxidizes in air. Copper is used for electrical wiring because it is a good conductor of electricity. Copper is used in the radiators of vehicles because it conducts heat. A sheet of copper is malleable and can be bent or shaped. That is why copper metal is used to make art imprints. Copper is also ductile and can be stretched.

The properties of nonmetals are generally opposite to the properties of metals.

GENERAL PROPERTIES OF NONMETALS

1. dull and brittle in the solid state
2. poor conductors of electricity
3. poor conductors of heat
4. non ductile
5. non malleable
6. exist as solids, liquids, or gases at room temperature

Sulfur is an example of a nonmetal.

Sulfur is a brittle, solid substance that has a dull surface. Because it is brittle, it cannot be bent and stretched into another shape. Sulfur is a nonconductor of electricity and heat.

By having properties that are the opposite of each other, metals and nonmetals can easily combine to form compounds.

Practice

Use the following information to answer the next question.

Shruti was required to make written observations on four substances displayed in her science class. The following chart shows some of the evidence she collected.

Substance	Evidence
1	Shiny, reddish solid; soft and bendable; conducts electricity
2	Grey-black solid; brittle; does not conduct electricity
3	Yellow, crumbly solid; does not conduct electricity
4	Dull, grey solid; bendable; conducts electricity

13. Which of the substances are **most likely** metals?

A. 1 and 2   **B.** 3 and 4

C. 2 and 3   **D.** 1 and 4

9.2.2.1a *"through investigations and applications of basic concepts: - demonstrate knowledge of laboratory, safety, and disposal procedures while conducting investigations"*

CONDUCTING INVESTIGATIONS

A science lab is a hands-on environment where students learn by doing. Therefore, it is important that all students follow certain safety guidelines associated with doing lab work. An understanding of how to use materials and equipment properly will help prevent accidents and ensure that the experiment is completed successfully.

These guidelines are particularly important in the areas of
- lab safety
- proper handling of materials
- emergency procedures

LAB SAFETY

There are basic lab safety rules that need to be followed when doing lab work. The checklist includes the following.

1. Become familiar with the experiment before starting on it.

2. Keep your work area uncluttered and organized.

3. Inform your teacher of any allergies or medical conditions you may have.

4. Always wear safety goggles and other protective equipment when handling chemicals or working with heat.

5. Remove jewellery, roll up long shirt sleeves, and tie long hair back.

6. Handle all glassware and chemicals carefully.

7. Do not touch or taste any materials unless instructed to do so by your teacher.

8. Become familiar with the chemical symbols on the containers.

9. Do not return unused chemicals to their original containers.

10. Place broken glassware in specially marked containers.

11. When heating glass containers, make sure you use heat-resistant Pyrex or Kimax glass containers.

12. When heating a liquid in a test tube, be sure to hold the test tube at an angle and point it away from yourself and others near your station.

13. Never smell any material directly. Instead, wave the air currents towards your nose.

14. Clean up your station after the experiment is finished and place all equipment and materials back in their proper places.

15. Always wash your hands with soap and water after completing the cleanup.

PROPER HANDLING OF MATERIALS

Many of the chemicals used for science experiments are potentially dangerous. It is required by law that the hazardous symbols appear on the label of a chemical container. Here are some of the labels that you may find on the materials used in your science classroom.

These eight symbols belong to a standard group called **WHMIS** or *Workplace Hazardous Materials Information System*.

Classification of Hazardous Materials (WHMIS)

Compressed Gas | Flammable and Combustible Material | Oxidizing Material | Poisonous and Infectious Material Materials Causing Immediate and Serious Toxic Effects

Poisonous and Infectious Material Materials Causing Other Toxic Effects | Biohazardous Infectious Material | Corrosive Material | Dangerously Reactive Material

Chemicals that have these hazardous symbols should be treated with care. The chemical residue and leftovers should be placed in a specially marked waste bucket. Your teacher will store the residue in plastic containers until such time that they can be picked up by a waste disposal company for proper disposal.

EMERGENCY PROCEDURES

Know the location of the *fire extinguisher*, *fire blanket*, and nearest *fire alarm*. Also know the location of the eye wash apparatus in your classroom.

In the case of an accident, notify your teacher as soon as possible. Follow your teacher's instructions if your assistance is required.

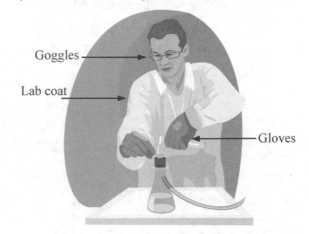

Goggles — Lab coat — Gloves

Use the following information to answer the next question.

It is not uncommon for scientists to discover bottles containing unknown liquids in their labs. One such bottle, labelled with a Workplace Hazardous Material Information System (WHMIS) symbol, is shown.

14. It is likely that the liquid in this bottle is

A. corrosive

B. flammable

C. an oxidizing agent

D. dangerously reactive

9.2.2.1b - *determine how the properties of substances influence their use*

PROPERTIES OF SUBSTANCES

All material has characteristic properties. These properties influence how and where the material is to be used.

In the past, it was more common to see a rusted vehicle than it is today. At one time, automobile manufacturers used steel to construct the body of a car. Steel has the property of oxidizing in air to form rust. This vehicle started to show signs of rust in a very short time.

In order to prevent premature rusting, the manufacturers of automobiles now use galvanized steel and plastic in the body construction. Galvanized steel is an alloy of steel and zinc and does not corrode as quickly as ordinary steel. Plastic is light and non-corrosive. As a result, automobile bodies last much longer before starting to rust out.

Alloys of metals are more commonly used today. An alloy is a metal that is blended with another metal or nonmetal to produce a product with properties that are more desirable.

An aircraft manufacturer uses a blend of aluminium, carbon fibre, and other metals to make the airplane's fuselage. This alloy material is lightweight, strong, malleable, and rust resistant.

The technology in the construction of golf clubs is also changing. Golf club heads and shafts are now made from an alloy of aluminium, steel, beryllium, and titanium. This alloy increases the strength and flexibility of the club, resulting in longer drives.

Hydrogen gas and helium gas are extremely light gas. You are about to send a balloon into the atmosphere to collect certain weather information.

Hydrogen gas and helium gas are both lighter than air. They will both cause the balloon to lift high into the atmosphere. Hydrogen gas, however, is extremely explosive and flammable. It is much safer to fill your weather balloon with helium gas.

It is mandatory that airbags be inserted in vehicles for safety reasons.

In order for airbags to work properly, they must inflate in a fraction of a second. A compound that has the property of producing a large volume of a safe gas is used. That compound is sodium azide (NaN_3). When a sensing device is activated during a collision, it closes an electrical circuit. The electrical current starts a chemical reaction that converts sodium azide into a large volume of nitrogen gas. This reaction inflates the airbag within 0.03 seconds.

Scientists choose specific materials and chemicals to obtain just the right results. They must consider the properties of the materials and chemicals before using them.

 Practice

Use the following information to answer the next question.

Romero constructs a simple circuit using a battery, a light bulb, and some wires. He uses wires made of various metals to check their electrical conductivity.

15. The light bulb glows **brightest** when the circuit is constructed using wires made from

A. iron B. silver

C. copper D. aluminium

9.2.2.1c - *formulate scientific questions about a problem or issue involving the properties of substances*

FORMULATING QUESTIONS ABOUT SUBSTANCE PROPERTIES

Scientists use properties to determine whether a substance is to be used for a particular purpose. For example, aluminium has properties (light, strong, corrosion resistant) that are better suited for the construction of an airplane fuselage than iron (heavy, strong, corrosive).

In this activity, students will use the properties table of pure substances to determine which properties make the substance best suited for the intended purpose.

Table Properties of Some Pure Substances

Pure Substance	Melting Point (°C)	Boiling Point (°C)	Density (g/cm³)	Appearance
ethanol (alcohol)	−115	78	0.8	clear, colourless liquid
aluminium	660	2 519	2.7	silvery-coloured solid
sodium bicarbonate (baking soda)	Decomposes rather than changes state	Decomposes rather than changes state	2.2	white solid
copper (II) sulfate (bluestone)	Decomposes rather than changes state	Decomposes rather than changes state	2.3	blue, solid crystals
carbon (diamond)	3 500	3 930	3.5	colourless solid crystals
carbon (graphite)	4 000	3 930	2.3	grey-black solid
copper	1 084	2 336	9.0	shiny reddish solid
glycerol (glycerine)	18	Decomposes rather than changes state	1.2	colourless, thick liquid
iron	1 535	3 000	7.9	grey solid
lead	327	1 750	1.3	blue-grey solid
sodium chloride (table salt)	801	1 465	2.2	white solid
calcium hydroxide (slaked lime)	Decomposes rather than changes state	Decomposes rather than changes state	2.2	white solid
sucrose (sugar)	170	Decomposes rather than changes state	1.6	white solid
sulfur	113	445	2.1	yellow solid
tin	232	2 270	7.3	silvery-yellowish solid
water	0	100	1.0	clear colourless, liquid

In Mr. Smith's science class, the students were challenged to determine the best answers and explanations for five questions. Students worked in groups and each group had to explain the answer to the question is based on the properties of substances listed in the chart.

:Example

Which pure substances are classified as elements and which are compounds?

Answer: The students had to know the definition of elements and compounds. An element is composed of only one type of substance. A compound is composed to two or more elements that are chemically combined. Aluminium, carbon copper, iron, lead, sulfur, and tin are elements. Ethanol, sodium bicarbonate, copper sulfate, sodium chloride, calcium hydroxide, sugar, and water are compounds.

:Example

Which substances are liquids at 6°C?

Answer: A substance exists in the liquid state between its melting point and its boiling point. Ethanol and water are liquids at 6°C. Glycerine remains a solid until 18°C.

:Example

James has a container of Substance X that has the following properties.
- Is a white solid
- Decomposes rather than changes state
- Is a liquid at 1 300°C

What is the name of Substance X?

Answer: Four substances are white solids: sodium bicarbonate, sodium chloride, calcium hydroxide, and sucrose. Three substances decompose at the boiling point, rather than change state. They are sodium bicarbonate, calcium hydroxide, and sucrose. The only white solid that is liquid at 1 300°C is sodium chloride.

:Example

Kayla has small containers of four substances: sugar, sulfur, sodium bicarbonate, and salt.

Which property would Kayla most likely use to quickly identify the container of sulfur?

A. Melting point

B. Density

C. Colour

D. State

Answer: The one property of the substances in the containers that stands out from the rest is colour. Sulfur is yellow, while the other three are white.

:Example

Samuel has a beaker of water. His task is to prove that the density of water in the beaker is $1.0 \, g/cm^3$. Describe the steps Samuel would take to prove this property.

Answer:
Step 1: Determine the volume of water in the beaker in mL.
Step 2: Determine the total mass of the water and its container.
Step 3: Pour the water into another container; dry the beaker and weigh it.
Step 4: Determine the mass of the water by subtracting the weight of the empty beaker from the combined weight of the beaker and the water.
Step 5: Divide the mass by the volume to determine the density.

9.2.2.1d - *demonstrate the skills required to plan and conduct an inquiry into the properties of substances, using apparatus and materials safely, accurately, and effectively*

SKILLS IN PLANNING AN INVESTIGATION

The students in Ms. Vallus's Grade 9 Science class are studying the properties of matter and are required to perform an experiment that will allow them to determine which substances are metals. Ms. Vallus indicated to the class that the steps in a scientific method had to be used to obtain their answers and proper safety guidelines had to be followed when performing the experiment.

What skills are important in order to plan and conduct this experiment?

Problem: To classify substances as metals based on physical properties.

The students are given five substances placed in dish-like containers. The substances are:

- Copper
- Iodine
- Aluminium
- Sulfur
- Zinc

What is important for the students to know in order to determine which substances are metals?

Students should have knowledge of the properties of metals and nonmetals.

Students should know the proper safety procedures for working with chemicals in the lab.

Students should use the scientific method approach to obtain an answer.

Again, emphasis has to be placed on making careful observations, recording data accurately, and working in a safe environment.

- Students should make a prediction or **hypothesis** on a possible outcome in this experiment.
- As part of the experimental **procedure**, students could attempt to stretch each substance (ductility), bend each substance (malleability), connect each substance in an electrical circuit to a light and cells, and mix each substance in a small amount of dilute hydrochloric acid.
- Students should list all the physical and chemical **observations** of each substance. Properties such as ductility, malleability, conduction of an electrical current, and reaction with dilute hydrochloric acid could be used.
- Students would then make a **conclusion** based on their observations. Finally, students would state an **application** of the results to an everyday situation.

Aluminium, copper, and zinc are ductile, malleable, conduct electricity, and react with hydrochloric acid to produce hydrogen gas. These three substances are metals. Sulfur and iodine are not ductile, not malleable, do not conduct electricity, and do not react with hydrochloric acid. They are nonmetals.

9.2.2.1e - *select and integrate information from various sources, including electronic and print resources, community resources, and personally collected data, to answer the questions chosen*

COLLECTING DATA

Research in science requires using different sources that will give **accurate** information about the topic you are collecting data for. Information can be found in books, on the Internet, or by asking experts in the field. More recent information can also be found in newspaper articles, periodicals, and brochures from government and business agencies.

CASE STUDY

Nathan knows that wastewater contains, grease, food particles, soap, and chemicals from cleaning products. He is curious to find out how these substances are removed during the wastewater treatment process.

To begin his research, Nathan decided to start with the Internet. He was able to obtain information on the stages of treatment at a wastewater facility. Nathan learned that wastewater treatment involves a physical process, a biological process, and a chemical process.

Nathan thought it might be a good idea to contact the Wastewater Treatment Facility to find out if they had any information on the chemical process involved in treating wastewater. The treatment facility did have pamphlets on the process. The receptionist at the facility suggested that Nathan speak to the person in charge of monitoring the chemical process. That person could give Nathan specific information on the removal of inorganic chemicals.

Nathan realized after conducting his research that most organic matter in wastewater is decomposed by the action of bacteria. Certain chemicals that may be present in wastewater, particularly those found in cleaning products, cannot be removed and are dumped back into rivers.

What can Nathan and his family do to reduce the number of inorganic chemicals in wastewater?

Obtaining information from several sources helped Nathan became aware of problems encountered when certain types of wastewater are dumped down the drain. As a result of his study, Nathan and his family decided to monitor what went down the drain and to reduce the number of commercial cleaning products they used.

Nathan's project involved the integration of several information sources to obtain reliable and accurate data.

9.2.2.1f - *organize, record, and analyse the information gathered*

RECORDING DATA FOR ANALYSIS

Doing scientific research requires that information be collected and recorded. The recorded data is then studied and analyzed. Finally, the data is organized in such a way that a conclusion is made. Consider the following example.

STUDENT ACTIVITY

Mr. Periodic, the science teacher, gave his class the names of three chemical substances and the symbols for three additional substances.

Names of Chemical Substances	Symbols for Chemical Substances
Water	$NaHCO_3$ (baking soda)
Sodium chloride (table salt)	H_2SO_4 (sulfuric acid)
Methane gas	C_3H_8 (propane gas)

The students were asked to determine the number of elements present in one molecule of each substance and the total number of atoms in that molecule. Students were then required to place the symbol of the substance in the correct box of the table provided.

How should the students approach this activity?

Step 1: Students have to figure out the chemical formula for the three named substances.

- water is H_2O
- sodium chloride is $NaCl$
- methane gas is CH_4

Step 2: Students are then required to figure out the number of elements and the total number of atoms present in the formula.

- H_2O 2 elements and 3 atoms
- $NaCl$ 2 elements and 2 atoms
- CH_4 2 elements and 5 atoms
- $NaHCO_3$ 4 elements and 6 atoms
- H_2SO_4 3 elements and 7 atoms
- C_3H_8 2 elements and 11 atoms

Step 3: Students must now take the analyzed information and organize it into the data table by placing the chemical formulae in the appropriate boxes.

Number of Elements

	1	2	3	4	5	6
2		NaCl				
3		H_2O				
4						
5		CH_4				
6				$NaHCO_3$		
7			H_2SO_4			
8						
9						
10						
11		C_3H_8				
12						
13						
14						

Number of Atoms (vertical axis label)

In order to obtain valid results, students must be able to gather information and process it in an organized way. At times, this may mean making a table of results and drawing a graph of the data in the table.

There are situations in which the data obtained has a pattern. The pattern can be the line on a line graph. The line graph below shows the temperature-time relationship when magnesium metal reacts with hydrochloric acid.

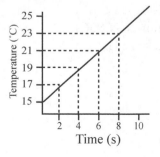

The temperature at five minutes is not indicated on the graph, but it can be determined by *interpolation*. Interpolation is predicting the result between two given points. The temperature at the five-minute mark is 22°C. Sometimes, a result can be determined by reading beyond the given data on a graph. Predicting a result beyond the given information is called *extrapolation*. The extrapolated value for 10 minutes is 25°C.

9.2.2.1g - *communicate scientific ideas, procedures, results, and conclusions using appropriate language and formats*

COMMUNICATING SCIENTIFIC IDEAS

Many situations in science occur where there is a need to communicate information. Communicating scientific ideas can occur through charts, tables, illustrations, and graphs.

A chart is a clear and concise way of comparing the physical and chemical properties of matter.

Substance	Scientific Name	Chemical Properties	Physical Properties
Dry ice	Carbon dioxide	Reacts with water to form acid rain	Gaseous state Very cold
Iodine	Iodine	Turns bluish-black in starch	Brown liquid
Glucose	Glucose	Produced when H_2O reacts with CO_2 in plant leaves	Sweet taste
Hydrogen gas	Hydrogen	Burns violently	Colourless gas

A graph is also is an effective way of comparing information.

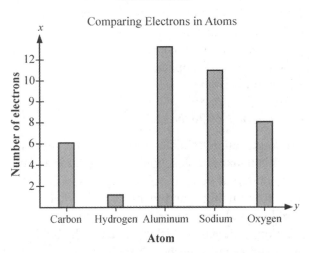

Comparing Electrons in Atoms

This graph compares the number of electrons in different atoms. It provides a visual that is easy to interpret. Aluminium has more electrons than any of the other atoms in the graph. The hydrogen atom has the fewest electrons.

9.2.2.2 *investigate, by laboratory experiment or classroom demonstration, the chemical properties of representative families of elements*

INVESTIGATING CHEMICAL PROPERTIES

Lithium, sodium, and potassium have similar properties. All three metals are extremely reactive with water. These elements are grouped in the same family in the periodic table. They belong to the alkali metals and are placed in Group 1.

Magnesium and calcium belong to the alkaline earth metals and are placed in the second family of elements. They belong to Group 2 and are less reactive with water.

Ms. Chemy, the Grade 9 Science teacher, chose magnesium and calcium metals to demonstrate to her class, that elements in the same family have similar properties. She placed a small piece of magnesium in one beaker of water and a similar-sized piece of calcium in another beaker of water. She asked the class to observe what happened.

The observations were the same for both magnesium and calcium:

- a white precipitate was formed
- bubbling and fizzing occurred
- red litmus paper turned blue

Ms. Chemy explained to her class that the reaction of magnesium and calcium first produced an oxide of the metal and hydrogen gas. Further reaction with the oxide and water produced a hydroxide. A hydroxide is a base, and any base turns red litmus blue.

Ms. Chemy wrote the word equation for these reactions on the board.

magnesium + water → magnesium oxide + hydrogen gas

magnesium oxide + water → magnesium hydroxide + hydrogen gas

calcium + water → calcium oxide + hydrogen gas

calcium oxide + water → calcium hydroxide + hydrogen gas

When Ms. Chemy added an acid to each metal, the class noticed bubbling. Hydrogen gas was produced.

Ms. Chemy also demonstrated to her class that magnesium and calcium will glow during a flame test. When heated over a Bunsen flame

- magnesium glows a brilliant white
- calcium glows a brick red

Magnesium and calcium have similar chemical properties. They therefore belong to the same family in the periodic table of elements.

Practice

16. Sodium reacts with water to

    A. displace carbon dioxide

    B. displace hydrogen

    C. produce nitrogen

    D. produce oxygen

9.2.2.3 *investigate the properties of changes in substances, and classify them as physical or chemical based on experiments*

PHYSICAL AND CHEMICAL CHANGES

PHYSICAL CHANGES

Physical changes can be made by altering:
- State—melting, freezing, boiling, or condensing
- Shape—cutting, breaking, or crushing
- Colour—as a result of dying or painting

A physical change occurs when matter changes its shape or state but retains its physical properties, or identity. For example, freezing water to make ice, simply changes the water's form. A change of state is a physical change. A physical change does not change the substance into another material. Ice is another form of water. It is not a new material. Another characteristic of a physical change is that it can be reversed. Ice can melt to form water again. It can then be frozen to make ice again. In another example, large pieces of copper can be heated and stretched into copper wire. During the change, the copper changes its physical appearance but keeps its identity. The type of matter has not changed, but its physical properties have changed.

CHEMICAL CHANGES

A chemical change is a change in matter that produces one or more new substances. The new substance(s) has properties that are different from the properties of the starting substance or substances. For example, fire is created when oxygen and wood react in the presence of heat. Ash and smoke are new substances created when wood is burned. It is important to note that a chemical change cannot be reversed. You cannot take ash from a fire and turn it back into wood.

Another example occurs when you apply heat to a raw egg. The egg cooks. The heat has caused a chemical change, and you cannot uncook the egg.

How can you tell when a chemical change or a chemical reaction has occurred? Scientists look for signs or evidence of a chemical change.
- A gas is produced
- The temperature changes
- A substance disappears
- A solid is formed
- Heat is given off
- A smell is produced

A good example of a chemical reaction happens when you take a tablespoon of baking soda and mix it into a cup of vinegar. If you try this, you should see a lot of bubbles and foam forming. These bubbles and foam are evidence of a chemical reaction. The gas that is produced in the bubbles and foam is called carbon dioxide.

A physical change does not affect the type of matter, but it will result in the matter having different physical properties. On the other hand, a chemical change will produce new matter with different characteristics from the original.

Practice

Use the following information to answer the next question.

A physical change is when a substance undergoes a change in its physical properties, such as colour, state, and density. A physical change does not involve a change in a substance's molecular structure, and so a new substance is not created. Normally, this change can be reversed via ordinary physical means.

17. Which of the following events is a physical change?
   A. Melting of ice
   B. Rusting of iron
   C. Burning of coal
   D. Burning of a candle

9.2.2.4 *construct molecular models of simple molecules*

CONSTRUCTING MOLECULAR MODELS

Many of the common substances you use every day are made up of simple compounds. To get a better understanding of these compounds, scientists build models of them. These models are useful because they represent what a molecule would look like if you were able to see it. The model can reveal useful information about a molecule by showing how many atoms of each element are present and how they are arranged.

For example, the chemical formula for water is H_2O. The letters represent elements found on the periodic table. The subscript number after the letter indicates how many atoms of that particular element are present in the compound. If no number is found after an element, it means there is only one atom of that element present. For water, the first letter, H, represents hydrogen. The subscript, two, that comes after indicates there are two hydrogen atoms present. The O represents oxygen. Because no number is found after the oxygen, it indicates that only one atom of oxygen is present.

To draw a molecule of water, simply place the oxygen in the centre and attach the two hydrogen molecules to it.

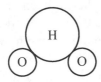

Oxygen is simply O_2, two oxygen molecules. They are represented below.

Ammonia has the chemical formula NH_3. There is one nitrogen atom surrounded by three hydrogen atoms.

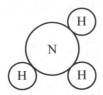

Methane, CH_4, is composed of one carbon atom surrounded by four hydrogen atoms.

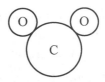

Carbon Dioxide, CO_2, can be drawn in the following manner.

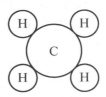

9.2.3.1 *identify uses of elements in everyday life*

ELEMENTS IN EVERYDAY LIFE

Iron is the most commonly used element on Earth. Iron can be mixed with other elements, such as carbon, to make stronger forms of iron, such as steel. Other elements that can be mixed to form different properties of steel are manganese and chromium. This results in steel that can be used for different purposes. For example, a tall building may need iron that does not bend. A car, however, may need iron that bends more easily.

Oxygen is also needed in the production of steel. Oxygen is used to burn off impurities such as carbon and phosphorous in the fabrication of steel, making it less brittle.

Oxygen is the most common element on Earth. It is found in air and water in the gaseous state. All living things need oxygen for cellular respiration, combustion, and decomposition. Oxygen is also needed for oxidation reactions, an example of which is burning. When oxygen mixes with other elements to form minerals, the mixture becomes a solid. Liquid oxygen is used as fuel for large rockets. Oxygen is also used when submarines need to surface, and for divers/climbers who need assistance breathing. Oxygen in its liquid form is used as fuel for large rockets.

Chlorine is almost always found mixed with other elements. When chlorine is by itself, it is a smelly and extremely poisonous gas. Chlorine is used in many cleaners, such as bleach. It is also used in swimming pools to kill germs.

Chlorine and sodium are often found joined together in nature. The two elements combine to make a mineral called halite, or rock salt. Rock salt is often used to melt ice on streets and sidewalks. Chlorine and sodium also form a different mineral that you use on your food, called table salt.

Carbon is one of the most important elements on Earth. It is found in every living thing. It can also mix with almost any other element.

There are a few minerals that are made of just carbon. Diamonds and graphite both contain only carbon. Even though they are made of the same element, they look very different from each other. This is because the carbon atoms in graphite are arranged differently than the carbon atoms in a diamond.

Aluminium is the most common metal in Earth's crust. Aluminium is very light, can be bent or shaped easily, but can become very strong when mixed with other elements. Most of the aluminium that is used today is a mixture of aluminium and other metals. Aluminium is used in vehicles, such as cars and bicycles. It is also used in cans, doors, and paints.

Practice

Use the following information to answer the next question.

Steel is formed by the combination of two or more elements. It is one of the most important forms of commercial iron.

18. Steel is an alloy that always contains the elements
    A. iron and carbon
    B. iron and copper
    C. calcium and iron
    D. chlorine and iron

9.2.3.2 *describe the methods used to obtain elements in Canada, and outline local environmental concerns and health and safety issues related to the ways in which they are mined and processed*

OBTAINING ELEMENTS IN CANADA

Elements in Canada such as gold, nickel, carbon, and uranium are mined in one of three major ways: surface mining, open-pit mining, or underground mining.

Surface mining occurs when the ore is removed from the immediate ground area. It is much safer for workers than underground mining, but it is much more damaging to the environment. Many mining companies try to restore surface mine sites after they have been closed. They replace the material they have dug out, replant native species of trees and other plants, and reintroduce animals to the area.

Open-pit mining is used when the deposit is near the surface, or when digging tunnels would be too dangerous. Open-pit mining creates many problems for the environment, such as large holes that can be over half a kilometre wide and hundreds of metres deep. Some of these holes are turned into landfills for disposing of solid wastes.

Underground mining is used when the deposit is located far below Earth's surface. A tunnel called a shaft is dug into the earth, and miners enter and physically remove the ore from deep under the ground. Underground mining may not appear to affect the surface of Earth, but it does in that waste material extracted from the ground is placed on the surface around the mine. This is especially hazardous when it occurs with uranium mining. Rainwater can then wash harmful materials from the rock into the ground or carry it to streams. Other times, abandoned mines can flood, which wears away rock, resulting in cave-ins. Not only does underground mining create problems for the Earth, but miners are at risk for respiratory problems, radiation sickness (from radioactive uranium), and cave-ins.

Once retrieved, the minerals can be processed in four major ways: milling, leaching, smelting, and in situ leach mining. Milling involves crushing the ore into a powder. Leaching is the process of adding an acid to separate the ore. This occurs in a physical plant. Smelting is using heat to separate the element from the ore. Nickel is processed in this way. In situ leach mining is a controversial method whereby a caustic agent is forced into the ground to dissolve the element that is to be removed. One of the major problems with this method is that the caustic agent leaches into the nearby soil, causing contamination of the ground and water table.

Mining is an important industry. Unfortunately, mining can have some harmful effects. Large areas of habitat for plants and animals can be lost. The local water can become polluted. This is dangerous for both people and animals. Mining companies need to make sure they do not permanently damage the environment.

Use the following information to answer the next question.

Mining is an important industry that also provides employment for many people in Canada. There are different types of mining, like open-pit mining. Open-pit mining is used when a mineral deposit is close to the surface of the Earth, or when digging tunnels would be too dangerous.

19. One environmental problem associated with open-pit mining is that

   A. the underground tunnels could cave in

   B. all of the ore is removed from the immediate ground area

   C. chemicals from underground tunnels get into water systems

   D. it creates holes on the surface that can be half a kilometre wide and hundreds of metres deep

9.2.3.3 *explain how a knowledge of the physical and chemical properties of elements enables people to determine the potential uses of the elements and assess the associated risks*

BENEFITS OF CHEMICAL KNOWLEDGE

Knowledge of the physical and chemical properties of elements enables people to determine the potential uses of the elements and assess the associated risks. For example, if the issue of copper versus aluminium wiring arose, one would need to compare the physical properties of ductility and conductivity. Which of these two elements is more apt to be stretched into a long wire and is a better conductor of electricity?

Chemical properties of elements are evaluated, for example, when helium versus hydrogen balloons are discussed. Some of the main issues are how do the two elements behave in air (hydrogen is lighter than helium) and how do they react to heat (helium is not flammable, hydrogen is). Once the answers to these questions are known, a decision can be made.

Another question could involve the discussion of copper versus lead in plumbing. Because water will probably be flowing through the pipes, one must look at each element and how it reacts with water and air. Health risks associated with the use of copper or lead should be taken into account. Additionally, some physical properties that must be assessed are the malleability and hardness of the elements.

Practice

Use the following information to answer the next question.

> Copper is a better choice than aluminium for the manufacture of air conditioners and various high efficiency electromagnetic devices. This is because aluminium magnetic wire needs to be thicker in diameter than copper magnetic wire.

20. Aluminium magnetic wire needs to be thicker in diameter than copper magnetic wires because of aluminium's

   A. higher electrical conductivity

   B. lower electrical conductivity

   C. higher specific heat

   D. lower specific heat

9.2.3.4 *identify and describe careers that require knowledge of the physical and chemical properties of elements and compounds*

CAREERS IN CHEMISTRY

Everything from creating chewing gum to the development of fuel for a space shuttle depends on chemistry. Those involved in this field are always searching for new information on how elements and compounds react by themselves and with other materials. There are a multitude of careers that require knowledge of the physical and chemical properties of elements and compounds.

1. Pharmaceutical researchers and medical chemists study the ways elements and compounds react with our bodies. In this way, safe medications are developed.

2. Chemical engineers create new synthetic products for industries.

3. Cosmetic scientists develop and research how cosmetics react to our bodies.

4. Perfume creators learn how elements and compounds combine to create smells in a stable, long-lasting form.

5. Pyrotechnicians combine chemicals to create safe and spectacular firework displays.

6. Organic chemists study carbon-based compounds. Many of these chemists work in the petroleum industry.

7. Material scientists research ways to create interesting materials with unique properties such as a lightweight, strong metal.

8. Forensic scientists use their knowledge of the properties of elements and compounds to solve crimes. They must be able to analyze evidence found at crime scenes.

9. Doctors, nurses, and pharmacists require knowledge of how medicinal drugs react in a person's body and what drugs to prescribe in specific situations.

10. A geochemist studies the chemical composition of Earth and other planetary bodies.

11. Food and flavour chemists create new ingredients and look for ways to enhance food. They also research better methods of processing, preserving, and storing food.

12. Hazardous-materials experts must understand how chemicals react and what to do in situations where hazardous chemicals have contaminated an area.

Practice

21. Which of the following professionals would require extensive knowledge of the physical and chemical properties of elements and compounds and their effects on humans?

   A. Physiotherapist   **B.** Pharmacist

   C. Technician   **D.** Architect

SOLUTIONS–CHEMISTRY: EXPLORING MATTER

1. D	6. OR	11. C	16. B	21. B
2. OR	7. B	12. B	17. A	
3. A	8. C	13. D	18. A	
4. OR	9. D	14. C	19. D	
5. D	10. OR	15. B	20. B	

1. D

Elements are the purest form of matter, and contain only one type of atom. Elements cannot be further subdivided into smaller particles by ordinary chemical means.

2. Open Response

An element is a pure substance that is made up of only one type of particle or atom. The element copper has only copper atoms and no other kind.

3. A

Compounds are pure substances formed when two or more elements combine chemically.

Therefore, sodium hydroxide is a compound because it is formed by the chemical combination of three elements: sodium, oxygen, and hydrogen.

$$Na_2O + H_2O \rightarrow 2NaOH$$
sodium oxide   water   sodium hydroxide

The individual properties of the elements are different from that of sodium hydroxide. Alternative A is correct.

4. Open Response

Passing electricity though water using a process called electrolysis causes the water molecule to break down into its elements, hydrogen and oxygen. The hydrogen and oxygen are in the form of two different gases.

5. D

When different atoms are combined, like in methane, they form molecules. Another common molecule is water. It is made up of two hydrogen atoms and one oxygen atom.

6. Open Response

A—Proton. This particle has a positive charge.
B—Neutron. This particle carries no charge.
C—Electron. This particle carries a negative charge.

7. B

Electrons, protons, and neutrons are the constituent particles of an atom. Of these, the entire negative charge is carried by electrons.

Distractor Rationale

A. Both protons and neutrons are present inside the nucleus.
C. Neutrons do not occupy the major portion of the nucleus: neutrons and protons are present in equal amounts.
D. Electrons are not present inside the nucleus; they are present outside the nucleus.
The correct answer is B.

8. C

While placing elements in a period in ascending order by atomic weight, Mendeleeff observed that chemically similar elements fall under the same vertical column. These vertical columns are called groups, and there are nine groups in the periodic table.

9. D

Fluorine (F) is in group 17, which is the halogen group, while Silicon (Si) is located along the staircase line in the periodic table, indicating it is a metalloid. The staircase line is located between metals and nonmetals on the periodic table and elements along it may have properties of metals or nonmetals

10. Open Response

NH_3

11. C

Baking soda is sodium hydrogen carbonate. The chemical formula of baking soda is $NaHCO_3$.
Distractor Rationale

A. $CaCO_3$ is the chemical formula for calcium carbonate (chalk).
B. Na_2CO_3 is the chemical formula for sodium carbonate (soda ash).
D. $Ca(OH)_2$ is the chemical formula for calcium hydroxide (slaked lime).

12. B

Sugar fermentation is an example of a chemical change. During fermentation, sugar changes into alcohol.

13. D

Metal have characteristic properties that are different from nonmetals. Metals tend to be shiny, malleable, ductile and conduct electricity. Non-metals generally are dull, brittle and do not conduct electricity. Substance 1 has all the characteristics of metals. Substance 4, although it is dull, is bendable and does conduct electricity. Substance 1 and Substance 4 have the characteristics of metals.

14. C

This question asks the student to recognize the appropriate meaning of the Workplace Hazardous Materials Information System (WHMIS) symbols. The symbols and their appropriate meanings are as follows.

Compressed Gas   Flammable and Combustible Material   Oxidizing Material   Poisonous and Infectious Material Materials Causing Immediate and Serious Toxic Effects

Poisonous and Infectious Material Materials Causing Other Toxic Effects   Biohazardous Infectious Material   Corrosive Material   Dangerously Reactive Material

Alternative C is correct.

15. B

Since silver has the highest electrical conductivity among metals, it is the best conductor of electricity. A light bulb glows brightest when a circuit is constructed using wires made from silver.

Distractor Rationale

A. The electrical conductivity of iron is less than that of silver, copper, and aluminium.

C. Although copper has high electrical conductivity, its conductivity is less than that of silver.

D. The electrical conductivity of aluminium is less than that of both copper and silver.

16. B

Sodium displaces hydrogen in water and releases energy. The reaction can be represented as:

$2Na + 2H_2O \Rightarrow 2NaOH + H_2 + energy$

This type of reaction is called a *single-displacement reaction.*

17. A

The melting of ice is a physical change because the liquid water formed from melting the ice can be turned back into ice simply by freezing it.

The rusting of iron, burning of a candle, and burning of coal are all chemical changes in which new products are formed, and these products cannot be turned back into the original iron, wax, and coal.

18. A

Steel is an alloy that always contains iron (Fe) and carbon (C). Other elements are sometimes added to steel to alter its properties, but it always contains iron and carbon.

19. D

An environmental problem likely to be associated with open-pit mining is that it can create holes that can be over half a kilometre wide and hundreds of metres deep. Open-pit mining does not require tunnels and is used when ore is close to the surface of the Earth but not in the immediate ground area.

20. B

Aluminium magnetic wires are larger than copper wires because of their lower electrical conductivity. Aluminium magnetic wires must be made in larger diameters to achieve the same linear conductivity as can be achieved by a smaller copper wire.

The correct answer is B.

21. B

Pharmacists require extensive training in chemistry so that they are aware of the physical and chemical properties of the chemicals they handle everyday. They also know which chemicals are dangerous to mix with others for prescriptions because of their effects on human body systems.

Unit Test

1. Which of the following substances is a pure substance that exists in the liquid state?
   A. Brass
   B. Oxygen
   C. Mercury
   D. Nitrogen

2. Which of the following statements about compounds is **true**?
   A. A compound has the same characteristics as its constituent elements.
   B. The elements of a compound can be separated by physical means.
   C. The elements in a compound lose their individual characteristics.
   D. A compound must contain at least three different elements.

3. Matter is made up of small individual particles called
   A. atoms
   B. compounds
   C. atoms and mixtures
   D. compounds and mixtures

4. With respect to their location in an atom, electrons are **best** described as
   A. occupying a large space surrounding the nucleus
   B. being evenly distributed throughout the nucleus
   C. being contained within the nucleus
   D. orbiting the atom

5. The elements in the modern periodic table are arranged
   A. alphabetically
   B. in increasing mass
   C. in increasing volume
   D. in increasing atomic number

6. The left-hand side of the periodic table contains **mainly**
   A. gases
   B. metals
   C. non-metals
   D. metalloids

Use the following information to answer the next question.

The composition of a compound is represented by its molecular formula, which indicates a compound's constituent elements and the proportion in which they are present in the compound.

7. The molecular formula of carbon dioxide is
   A. C_2H_2
   B. CH_4
   C. CO_2
   D. CO

8. Which of the following phenomena is a chemical change?
   A. Freezing of ice to water
   B. Evaporation of ethanol for cooling
   C. Crystallization of a soluble salt from water
   D. Carbon reacting with oxygen to give carbon dioxide

Use the following information to answer the next question.

Four Properties of Metals and Non-Metals	
Metals	**Non-Metals**
Shiny	Dull
Ductile	Brittle
Conductors of electricity	Non-Conductors of electricity

9. According to the properties listed in the table, which of the following elements is classified as a non-metal?
   A. Zinc
   B. Sulfur
   C. Copper
   D. Aluminium

Open Response

10. What are six properties of non-metals?

_____
_____
_____
_____
_____

11. Which of the following practices will promote safety during scientific experiments?

   A. Controlling variables and knowing the safety symbols

   B. Following scientific methods and using a large sample size

   C. Knowing how to use scientific equipment and having a control

   D. Following instructions and understanding the purpose of an experiment

12. Which of the following gases should be used to fill a blimp so that it can safely fly?

   A. Hydrogen   B. Nitrogen

   C. Oxygen   D. Helium

   Use the following information to answer the next question.

   Luke is designing an experiment to test the conductivity of various substances.

13. Which of the following substances should **not** be used in this experiment?

   A. Sulfur   B. Copper

   C. Silver   D. Zinc

14. Which of the following processes does **not** involve a chemical change?

   A. Burning   B. Cooking

   C. Melting   D. Rusting

Open Response

Use the following information to answer the next question.

Mrs. Wilkins is demonstrating the difference between physical changes and chemical changes to her grade six class. She is holding a piece of paper in her hand, and she asks the class to suggest what she could do to the paper to demonstrate a physical change and then a chemical change. Jerry puts up his hand and offers two suggestions.

15. What procedures could Jerry suggest that would demonstrate a physical change to the paper and a chemical change to the paper?

   _____
   _____
   _____
   _____
   _____
   _____
   _____
   _____

Use the following information to answer the next question.

Water technologists have developed a program to ensure that drinking the water supplied by a sewage treatment plant is safe to drink and free of microorganisms. A chemical is added to the water during the water treatment process to ensure its safety.

16. During the water treatment process, the chemical that is added to water to control unsafe microorganisms is

   A. nitrate   B. fluorine

   C. chlorine   D. phosphate

SOLUTIONS

1. C	5. D	9. B	13. A
2. C	6. B	10. OR	14. C
3. A	7. C	11. D	15. OR
4. A	8. D	12. D	16. C

1. C

According to the particle theory of matter, pure substances are made up of identical particles. Mercury, which exists in the liquid state, is a pure substance that contains only one kind of particle.

A. Brass is an alloy of copper and zinc. Hence, it is a mixture.

B. Oxygen is a pure substance, but it exists in the gaseous state.

D. Nitrogen is a pure substance, but it exists in the gaseous state.

2. C

The elements in a compound lose their individual characteristics. For example, both hydrogen and oxygen are combustible substances. When combined as water, they can extinguish fire.

3. A

According to the particle theory of matter, matter is made up of small particles called atoms.

The correct answer is A.

4. A

The atom consists of a tiny nucleus containing positively charged protons and uncharged neutral neutrons. Negatively charged electrons occupy a large space surrounding the nucleus, which is sometimes referred to as an "electron cloud."

Alternative B is incorrect. The electrons are not distributed throughout the entire atom evenly, since they are not contained within the nucleus.

Alternative C is incorrect because electrons are not contained within the nucleus.

Alternative D is incorrect because electrons are contained within the atom, not orbiting it.

5. D

After Mendeleev's periodic table was formulated, he discovered that the properties of the elements are related more to their atomic numbers than their atomic weights. Hence, the periodic law of the modern table states: "The physical and the chemical properties of the elements are periodic functions of their atomic numbers."

6. B

The elements present on the left-hand side of the periodic table have large atomic sizes and few valance electrons. These elements are electropositive in nature and lose electrons quite easily to form positive ions. These elements are mostly metals.

The correct answer is B.

7. C

Carbon dioxide is made up of two elements: carbon (C) and oxygen (O). It contains one atom of carbon and two atoms of oxygen. Hence, the molecular formula for carbon dioxide is CO_2.

C_2H_2 is the molecular formula for ethane.

CH_4 is the molecular formula for methane.

CO is the molecular formula for carbon monoxide.

8. D

Evaporation, crystallization, and freezing are physical changes, not chemical reactions. Carbon reacting with oxygen to yield carbon dioxide is a chemical change.

9. B

Sulfur is dull, does not conduct electricity, and is brittle, indicating that it is a non-metal.

10. Open Response

Non-metals are dull and brittle, they poor conductors of electricity, and they are poor conductors of heat. Non-metals are non-ductile, non-malleable, and exist as solids, liquids, and gases at room temperature.

11. D

Instructions are used to outline the correct and safest way to use equipment and conduct experiments. Following them carefully promotes safety. Understanding the purpose of an experiment means that the experimenter knows what they will be doing in the lab and what equipment they will be using. This minimizes risks. Without a clear understanding of the purpose of an experiment, the experimenter cannot identify dangers and plan ways to reduce them.

Controlling variables, using a large sample size, following scientific methods, and having a control ensure the accuracy and credibility of experiment rather than safety. Knowing the safety symbols and how to use scientific equipment promote safety, but these procedures were paired with procedures that promote accuracy and reliability of experiments.

12. D

Helium is the safest gas to fill the blimp with because of its inertness. It is more stable than the other elements listed and is very inactive.

13. A

Sulfur should not be used, since it is classified as a non-metal and therefore is not a good conductor. Luke would have to choose another metal to have four usable substances.

14. C

Melting is the process in which the state of matter of a substance changes from a solid to a liquid. The chemical properties of the substance do not change during this process, so it is a physical change.

Burning, cooking, and rusting all involve the production of new substances. The chemical properties of substances change during burning, cooking, or rusting.

The correct answer is C.

15. Open Response

The paper could be physically changed by a change of shape. This could be accomplished by cutting the paper into smaller pieces, or by crushing the paper into a ball. The paper might also be allowed to soak in water until it breaks apart into wood fibre. Since the wood fibre could be arranged back in to a sheet of paper, this process is reversible and counts as a physical change.

The paper would be changed chemically if it was burned, or if it was exposed to some acid or other chemical that reacted with the paper, resulting in a colour change, the release of heat energy, or the production of a gas. These are all indicators that a chemical change has taken place. The materials that remain after a chemical reaction has taken place cannot be made back into paper again. These processes cannot be reversed.

16. C

Chlorine and fluorine are both added to drinking water; however, only chlorine is added in order to kill microorganisms.

Space Exploration

Earth and Space Science: Space Exploration

Table of Correlations

Specific Expectation		Practice Questions	Unit Test Questions
9.3.1	Understanding Basic Concepts		
9.3.1.1	*recognize and describe the major components of the universe using appropriate scientific terminology and units*	1, 2, 3	1, 2
9.3.1.3	*describe, compare, and contrast the general properties and motions of the components of the solar system*	7, 8, 9	4, 5
9.3.1.4	*describe the sun and its effects on the Earth and its atmosphere*	10, 11, 12	6
9.3.1.5	*describe and explain the effects of the space environment on organisms and materials*	13, 14	7
9.3.1.2	*describe the generally accepted theory of the origin and evolution of the universe (i.e., the "big bang" theory) and the observational evidence that supports it*	4, 5, 6	3
9.3.2	Developing Skills of Inquiry and Communication		
9.3.2.1a	*through investigations and applications of basic concepts: - identify problems and issues that scientists face when investigating celestial objects and describe ways these problems can be solved*	15	8
9.3.2.1c	*demonstrate the skills required to plan and conduct an inquiry about space exploration, using instruments, tools, and apparatus safely, accurately, and effectively*	16	9
9.3.2.1d	*select and integrate information from various sources, including electronic and print resources, community resources, and personally collected data, to answer the questions chosen*		
9.3.2.1e	*organize, record, and analyze the information gathered*		
9.3.2.1f	*communicate scientific ideas, procedures, results, and conclusions using appropriate SI units, language, and formats*		
9.3.2.2	*conduct investigations on the motion of visible celestial objects, using instruments, tools, and apparatus safely, accurately, and effectively*	17	10, 11
9.3.2.3	*gather, organize, and record data through regular observations of the night sky and/or use of appropriate software programs, and use these data to identify and study the motion of visible celestial objects*		
9.3.2.1b	*formulate scientific questions about a problem or issue in space exploration*		
9.3.3	Relating Science to Technology, Society, and the Environment		
9.3.3.1	*identify and assess the impact of developments in space research and technology on other fields of endeavour*	18	12, 13
9.3.3.3	*provide examples of the contributions of Canadian research and development to space exploration and technology*	21, 22	15
9.3.3.4	*explore careers in science and technology that are related to the exploration of space, and identify their educational requirements*	23, 24	16
9.3.3.2	*relate the beliefs of various cultures concerning celestial objects to aspects of their civilization*	19, 20	14

9.3.1.1 *recognize and describe the major components of the universe using appropriate scientific terminology and units*

COMPONENTS OF THE UNIVERSE

The universe is all the matter and energy that exists around us. It spans billions of light years and is currently expanding. The universe is made up of many different forms of matter, including galaxies, stars, nebulas, planets, comets, and asteroids.

It is hard to think about the size and emptiness of space. If the sun were a model with a diameter of one metre, Earth would be the size of a marble orbiting about 100 metres from the sun. Saturn would be the size of a golf ball orbiting one kilometre away. Neptune, the most distant planet, would orbit 3 kilometres from the sun. Using the same model, the nearest star would be 29 000 kilometres away from the sun.

Ordinary units like kilometres and miles are too small for astronomical distances. The distance between the planets is measured using the astronomical unit (AU). One AU is approximately equal to 146.9 million km, which is the average distance from the sun to Earth.

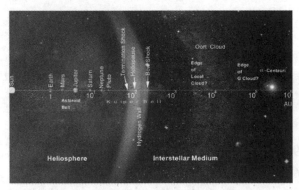

Distances of the solar system measured using astronomical units (AU).

The distance from the sun to Saturn is 9.5 AU; from the sun to Neptune is 30 AU. The farthest edge of the solar system, the Oort cloud, stretches out 50 000 AU from the sun.

Astronomical units very quickly become too small to use for interstellar distances. For even greater distances, astronomers use the light year (ly). One light year is the distance light travels in one year. Since the speed of light is 300 000 kilometres per second (186 000 miles per second), in one year, light can travel about 9.5 trillion kilometres (5.9 trillion miles, 63 240 AU). The next nearest star to Earth is Proxima Centauri, over 271 000 AU from the sun, 4.22 light years away. The Milky Way galaxy, which contains Earth's solar system, is about 100 000 light years in diameter, so it would take 100 000 years to cross it at the speed of light. The Milky Way galaxy consists of several spiral arms and is referred to as a spiral galaxy. The four major spiral arms of the Milky Way are the Perseus arm, the Norma and Cygnus arm, the Crux and Scutum arm, and the Carina and Sagittarius arm. A small spiral arm known as the Orion arm exists between the Perseus arm and the Carina and Sagittarius arm. Earth's solar system lies at the inner rim of the Orion arm.

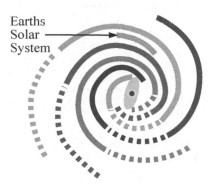

Earths Solar System

Milky Way Galaxy

Other types of galaxies can be barred, elliptical, and irregular in shape. Andromeda is the nearest galaxy to the Milky Way, 2.5 million light years away.

The distances between galaxies are measured in light years (and parsecs). Galaxies range anywhere from tens of thousands to six or seven million light years away. The edge of the universe that scientists can currently observe is about 14 billion light years from Earth.

Practice

Open Response

1. Sometimes, scientists provide estimates rather than actual measurements. For example, many scientists make estimates about the distance between our galaxy and other galaxies rather than giving an exact measurement.

Explain why scientists would provide estimates about distances in space rather than exact measurements.

_____

_____

_____

_____

_____

_____

_____

_____

Use the following information to answer the next question.

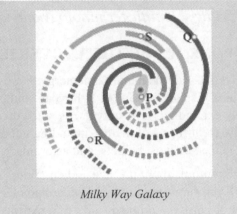

Milky Way Galaxy

2. A schematic diagram of four points in the Milky Way galaxy is shown in the given figure. The position of our solar system in the Milky Way galaxy is represented by point

   A. P   **B.** Q   **C.** R   **D.** S

3. When units are arranged in order from shortest to longest, they are

   A. kilometre, light year, astronomical unit

   B. kilometre, astronomical unit, light year

   C. astronomical unit, kilometre, light year

   D. light year, astronomical unit, kilometre

9.3.1.2 *describe the generally accepted theory of the origin and evolution of the universe (i.e., the "big bang" theory) and the observational evidence that supports it*

THE ORIGIN OF THE UNIVERSE

Astronomers have believed for a long time that the universe was created by a large explosion. During this creation, matter was formed from finer particles and was sent flying in all directions. As the matter cooled, it began to form clouds of molecules that eventually joined together to form stars and planets.

This theory came into existence through observations of galaxies. They appear to be flying out from a central position and expanding. Scientists have also observed a redshift in stars. As a result of increasing distances between stars, the wavelengths of light travelling from the stars toward Earth shift toward the higher red light wavelength. Measurements of this expansion indicate that the big bang occurred 13 to 14 billion years ago.

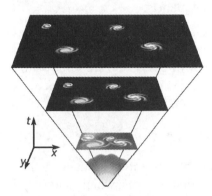

The universe expanding

During the 18th century, Immanuel Kant and Pierre Laplace proposed a model for the formation of the solar system called the nebula theory. A swirling cloud of gas and dust came together, and over time, more gas, dust, and rocks were pulled into the centre of the cloud as density increased. As mass increased, so did the gravitational pull of an object.

This progression occurred throughout space. As more matter was pulled in, the speed of this process increased. This system began to spin, and in the process, the central core flattened into a disk shape. This is how our galaxy, the Milky Way, was formed.

As the density of the core increased, so did the pressure and temperature. As a result, nuclear fission began and our Sun was created.

Many of the smaller pieces of rock, gas, and dust came together to form protoplanets, or future planets. As the mass of the object became larger, it attracted more debris. Sometimes, many protoplanets collided to form a single object, or larger planet. It is believed that the larger planets, Jupiter, Saturn, Neptune, and Uranus, are failed stars, because their composition is close to that of the sun (hydrogen and helium) and also because they are large in size. Gravity eventually took over and made these future planets spherical in shape.

Many scientists believe that moons, meteors, asteroids, and comets are leftover pieces of rock, gas and debris that did not become a planet. Some are believed to be pieces of planets that have fallen off after collisions with other planets or are leftovers from an explosion.

PROBLEMS WITH THIS THEORY

Although the big bang theory is generally accepted, there are problems with it.

1. The theory does not state what came before the big bang. It suggests that time itself was created at the big bang, and the theory cannot account for anything before this.

2. The theory has little information about the part of the universe that scientists are unable to observe. If the big bang occurred about 14 billion years ago, anything farther than 14 billion light years from Earth cannot be observed. The big bang tries to explain only the observable universe.

3. The big bang is often described as an explosion. It is more like the appearance of the entire universe followed by a rapid expansion. It is the space between stars that is expanding, not the stars themselves.

Practice

| Open Response |

Use the following information to answer the next question.

Scientists have discovered that the universe is expanding by studying stars, and in particular the redshift of these stars.

4. What is redshift of a star? How does the redshift of a star show that the universe is expanding?

_____

_____

_____

_____

_____

5. The big bang theory, which states that the universe began 13 to 14 billion years ago with a massive explosion, is supported by

   A. the presence of big, luminous stars

   B. evidence of the expanding universe

   C. the presence of rotating celestial bodies

   D. evidence of the rotations of celestial bodies

6. According to the Big Bang theory, the universe was born as a result of a

   A. big explosion

   B. violent electrocution

   C. huge stellar collision

   D. steady flow of energy

9.3.1.3 *describe, compare, and contrast the general properties and motions of the components of the solar system*

PROPERTIES AND MOTIONS OF THE SOLAR SYSTEM

The solar system consists of the sun and all of the objects that revolve around it. There are eight planets that revolve around the sun, as well as dwarf planets, many moons, and countless meteoroids, asteroids, and comets. All of the objects in space are held in a specific orbiting path by the force of gravity. The speed and distance each object moves depends on its individual characteristics. The objects that orbit the sun are held in elliptical orbits.

The solar system is incredibly large. It is estimated that all of the objects within the solar system stretch across a diameter of approximately 10 trillion km.

PLANETS

The eight planets revolving around the sun are divided into the inner planets and the outer planets. The inner and outer planets are divided by an asteroid belt between Mars and Jupiter.

The inner planets are Mercury, Venus, Earth, and Mars. They are smaller in size and are composed of rocky material. These planets are referred to as the rocky, or terrestrial planets.

The outer planets are Jupiter, Saturn, Uranus, and Neptune. They are larger than the inner planets, are composed primarily of gases, and are referred to as the gas giants, or Jovian planets. These planets take longer to orbit the sun than the inner planets.

DWARF PLANETS

Currently there are also five dwarf planets in the solar system. The first is Ceres, which is located in the asteroid belt between Mars and Jupiter. Pluto is located past Neptune, although occasionally their orbits change so that Neptune is farther from the sun. Pluto was once considered the ninth planet of the solar system; however, scientists have recently re-classified Pluto because of its size. Haumea is located past Pluto, and Makemake is located past Haumea. Eris is located farther out past Makemake and is the farthest planet from the sun. It takes Eris 557 years to complete one revolution around the sun.

As of September 18, 2008, only five objects have been classified as dwarf planets. It is predicted that more will be found as scientists study the Kuiper Belt at the outer edge of our solar system and beyond. Astronomers measure the distances of objects in the solar system using the astronomical unit (AU). One AU is the measurement of the distance from Earth to the sun. By comparison, the distance from Mercury to the sun is 0.39 AU, and the distance from Neptune to the sun is 30.06 AU.

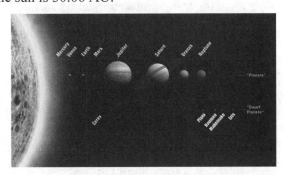

The solar system

Each planet has its own unique features and characteristics. The following chart compares some of these characteristics:

Planet	Distance from Sun (AU)	Number of Moons	Average Surface Temperature (°C)	Period of Orbital Revolution
Mercury	0.39	0	180	88 days
Venus	0.72	0	480	225 days
Earth	1	1	15	365.25 days
Mars	1.52	2	−53	607 days
Jupiter	5.27	28	−180	11.9 years
Saturn	9.54	19	−180	29.5 years
Uranus	19.19	17	−214	84 years
Neptune	30.06	8	−220	165 years

THE MOONS

Moons are naturally occurring satellites that orbit the planets. Earth has only one moon, while Jupiter has 63. Venus and Mercury have no moons at all.

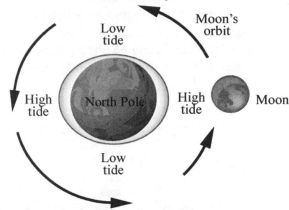

Moons affect the planets that they orbit. The moon orbiting Earth affects the tides of Earth's oceans. The position of the moon above Earth's surface determines whether the tide is high or low.

ROCKY FRAGMENTS

There are fragments of rock in the solar system that are too small to be planets; however, these fragments also revolve around the sun in their own orbits. These fragments can be classified as asteroids or meteoroids, depending on their size.

The larger rocky fragments in the solar system are called **asteroids**. They are the rocky debris left over from the formation of the solar system. Most asteroids are found in the main asteroid belt in the solar system, which is located between Mars and Jupiter. The largest object in the asteroid belt is Ceres, which is approximately 940 km across. It has recently been classified as a dwarf planet, similar to Pluto.

There are smaller fragments of rock in the solar system. These are called **meteoroids**. Occasionally, these smaller fragments are pulled toward Earth by gravity. Meteoroids that enter the Earth's atmosphere are called **meteors**. Friction caused by the movement of the meteor through the atmosphere causes the rocks to heat up. As a result, they can be seen by an observer on Earth as streaks of light, or a meteor shower. Sometimes, these burning meteors are called shooting stars. The meteors may burn up in the atmosphere, or they might fall to Earth's surface as **meteorites**.

COMETS

Comets consist mostly of ice, gas, and dust. They also travel in elliptical orbits around the sun. As a comet approaches the sun, it begins to warm up. Some of the ice will begin to melt, releasing dust and gas into space. The dust and gas form a visible tail behind the comet that can be observed on Earth at night. These tails can stretch out millions of kilometres in length.

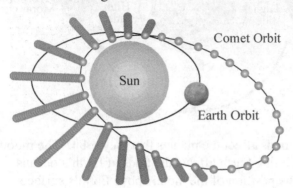

Since comets have a regular orbit around the sun, their reappearance is predictable. For example, Halley's Comet is visible from Earth every 76 years. It will next appear in 2033. Other comets, like Hale-Bopp, which passed closest to Earth in 1997, will not be seen again until 4377.

 Practice

Open Response

7. Tides are changes in water levels in oceans. Tides change four times in a 24-hour period. How does the relationship between the moon and Earth result in low and high tides?

_____

_____

_____

_____

_____

_____

_____

Use the following information to answer the next question.

Planet	Distance from the Sun (AU)	Period of Rotation	Period of Orbital Revolution
Earth	1.00	23.93 h	365.25 days
Mercury	0.39	59 days	88 days
Jupiter	5.27	9.85 h	11.9 years
Neptune	30.06	16.2 h	165 years
Venus	0.72	243 days	225 days

8. Which of the following statements presents a valid comparison of the data in the above table?

A. The rotation period has no effect on the orbital revolution period.

B. As the rotation period increases, the orbital revolution period increases.

C. As the distance from the sun decreases, the rotation period increases.

D. As the distance from the sun decreases, the orbital revolution period increases.

Use the following information to answer the next question.

No human has ever been to Pluto. Scientists believe that if astronauts made it past Pluto's orbit, they would find large clouds of particles. This region is thought to be home to long-period comets.

9. What is the name of this cloudy region?

A. The Galileo cloud

B. The Hubble cloud

C. The Solar cloud

D. The Oort cloud

9.3.1.4 *describe the sun and its effects on the Earth and its atmosphere*

THE SUN AND ITS RELATIONSHIP TO THE EARTH

The sun is just one star among millions in the Milky Way galaxy. It is the only star in our solar system, and it is located near the centre of the solar system. Compared to other stars, the sun is average size; however, compared to other objects in the solar system, it is massive. It is 109 times bigger than Earth. One million Earths could fit into the sun. The sun has a diameter of 1 392 000 km. Its mass makes up 98% of the total mass of the solar system.

The sun is about halfway through its life. It is about 4 to 5 billion years old, and will exist for another 4 to 5 billion years. The sun is basically a large ball of super-heated gases. Its surface temperature is around 6 000°C. Inside the sun, the temperature is nearly 16 000 000°C. The sun is made up mainly of hydrogen gas. This hydrogen gas is changed into helium gas by the process of fusion. This change creates most of the sun's energy.

The sun

ENERGY FROM THE SUN

Energy from the sun and other objects in space comes in various forms.

The sun's energy appears to us as visible white light. In addition, the sun gives off invisible infrared light and ultraviolet light that can only be felt, not seen.

- Visible light—The band of rainbow colours seen with a prism are different electromagnetic waves. All of these colours combined make sunlight appear white. This is the visible portion of the sun's energy.
- Infrared light—This energy is not visible to the human eye. This is the portion of the sun's energy that heats the Earth.
- Ultraviolet light—This energy is not visible to the human eye. A relatively small portion of the sun's energy is ultraviolet light waves. The human body uses ultraviolet light to produce vitamin D. Too much ultraviolet light causes sunburn.

Other forms of energy are emitted by objects in space. These include radio waves, microwaves, X-rays, and gamma rays.

All of the energy released by the sun and other objects in space belongs to the electromagnetic spectrum.

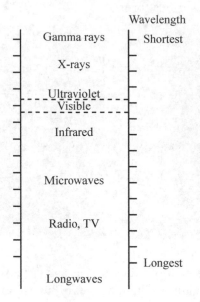

A solar flare just below the dark sunspot

PHOTOSYNTHESIS

Except for ecosystems in caves and in the deep sea, all life on Earth relies on energy from the sun. Green plants, algae, and some bacteria convert the sun's energy into chemical energy. The process by which sunlight is converted into chemical energy in food is referred to as photosynthesis. The food made by plants provides energy for all animal life on Earth.

SOLAR ACTIVITY

Activity on the sun affects life on Earth. The sun is a burning ball of gas and may occasionally produce solar flares. A solar flare is an explosion that releases a large amount of electromagnetic radiation. This explosion usually happens around dark spots that are a lower temperature than their surroundings. These areas are known as sunspots.

The energy released during a solar flare can cause disruptions in communication systems on Earth. The release of large amounts of energy interferes with the frequency signals used by radar and signal transmitters on satellites.

Solar flares also create solar winds. The solar winds travel through space and eventually reach the Earth's atmosphere. When the solar winds collide with the particles in the Earth's atmosphere, they produce a phenomenon called aurora borealis.

AURORA BOREALIS

Aurora borealis, or northern lights, is a naturally occurring display of dancing colours that can be seen in the night sky. This display normally happens above the Earth's north and south polar regions.

Northern lights

Why does the aurora borealis occur? Solar winds carry charged particles into the Earth's atmosphere. These particles collide with the Earth's magnetosphere (the atmosphere above the magnetic North Pole) to produce electromagnetic radiation that is visible in different colours. During peak solar activity, the aurora borealis can be seen in the southern part of Canada and northern United States.

Practice

Open Response

Use the following information to answer the next question.

> Aurora borealis, or the northern lights, is a naturally occurring display of dancing colours seen in the night sky above Earth's north and south polar regions.

10. Why does aurora borealis occur?

_____

_____

_____

_____

_____

11. In the electromagnetic spectrum, visible light lies between

   A. ultraviolet rays and infrared rays

   B. infrared rays and radio waves

   C. microwaves and radio waves

   D. gamma rays and X-rays

12. A continuous stream of charged particles, originating from the sun's corona, flows outward through the solar system. The flow of these charged particles is known as a

   A. solar storm   **B.** solar wind

   C. maelstrom   **D.** solar flux

9.3.1.5 *describe and explain the effects of the space environment on organisms and materials*

THE CHALLENGES OF LIVING IN SPACE

When astronauts are in space, their bodies undergo many changes as they adjust to living in microgravity. **Microgravity** is a condition in which the normal forces of gravity are greatly reduced. In space, an astronaut becomes almost weightless. Weightlessness can confuse the body's senses and alter the normal functioning of the organs.

Astronauts experience weightlessness in a microgravity environment.

Gravity tends to pull downwards on the body. This is what the astronaut on Earth is accustomed to. In space, the gravitational force on the body is greatly reduced. As a result, several things occur physically.

- Fluids move from the legs to the upper body and head. This extra fluid can create a 'puffy face' look.
- Bones start to deteriorate and become less dense.
- Backbone stretches and may cause severe back pain.
- Muscles lose their tone and become weaker.
- Balance and orientation are distorted.
- Motion sickness and nausea occur.

When an astronaut comes back to Earth, it usually takes several weeks before his or her body returns to normal.

Exercising in space

An astronaut in space also faces other challenges. There is very little room to move on a spacecraft. Living spaces are shared among the members of the crew. Psychologically, it can become difficult to live and work with the same people day after day in crowded conditions. It can also be difficult to get accustomed to eating and sleeping in a space environment. Even going to the bathroom can present challenges.

One important piece of equipment used by astronauts is the space suit. The space suit is designed to protect the astronauts from radiation and extreme temperatures. An astronaut's suit is made of several insulated layers and is pressurized for comfort. At the same time, the suit must be flexible to allow the astronaut freedom to move around.

An astronaut's space suit is designed for safe travel in space.

A spacecraft is small and has limited room. It is impossible to carry a large supply of water and oxygen. Almost all space shuttles carry devices that can recycle water. Wastewater and moisture from the cabins is collected, distilled, and reused. A small supply of water for emergency use is carried in storage tanks.

Sometimes, oxygen is removed from wastewater by the process of electrolysis. An electrical device is used to decompose water into oxygen gas and hydrogen gas. Oxygen gas is stored and hydrogen gas is vented out of the spacecraft. Oxygen that is carried on the spacecraft is stored as a liquid in pressurized containers. Liquid oxygen takes up much less space than oxygen gas.

Food carried onboard a spacecraft is dehydrated. Removing the water makes the food item much lighter. The smaller package requires less space to store.

Helping to keep more people healthier longer

York's Faculty of Health will help you gain a deeper understanding of people. Our health and human science programs range from the molecular to the global. We'll provide you with insights into the broader factors determining the health of individuals, countries and whole populations.

School of Health Policy & Management
The only school of its kind. Explore health from an interdisciplinary perspective. The Honours Bachelor of Health Studies (BHS degree) is offered in Health Management, Health Informatics and Health Policy.

School of Kinesiology & Health Science
Study human movement and the relationship between physical activity and health. We offer both the Bachelor of Arts (BA) and Bachelor of Science (BSc) degrees.

School of Nursing
Patient centered learning in a dynamic and collaborative setting. Earn a Bachelor of Science (BScN) in Nursing.

Psychology
Canada's largest selection of psychology courses offered by world renowned educators and researchers. Both three and four-year degrees are offered including the Bachelor of Arts (BA) and Bachelor of Science (BSc).

Visit www.yorku.ca/health or Call at 416 736-5124

YORK UNIVERSITÉ UNIVERSITY U50

redefine THE POSSIBLE.

We don't have all the answers.

Just more answers than any other university in Canada.

With more world-leading researchers, in more fields, teaching 841 distinct undergraduate, 520 graduate and 42 professional programs, U of T is Canada's leader in answering the world's toughest questions. And we're educating this country's brightest to do the same.

UNIVERSITY OF
TORONTO
www.utoronto.ca

CANADA'S ANSWERS TO THE WORLD'S QUESTIONS.

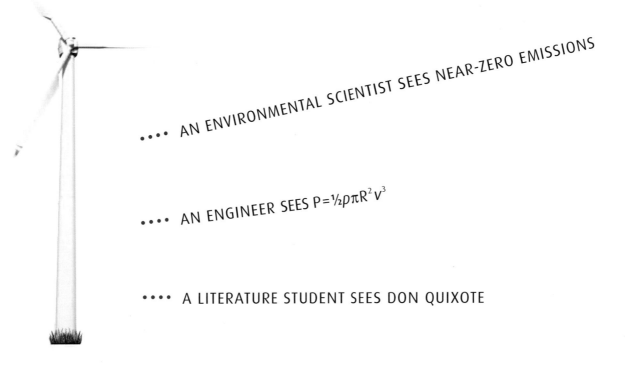

.... AN ENVIRONMENTAL SCIENTIST SEES NEAR-ZERO EMISSIONS

.... AN ENGINEER SEES $P = \frac{1}{2}\rho\pi R^2 v^3$

.... A LITERATURE STUDENT SEES DON QUIXOTE

QUESTION EVERY ANGLE.
STUDY EVERY ANGLE.
RESEARCH EVERY ANGLE.

WELCOME TO THE INTERDISCIPLINARY UNIVERSITY. At York, we tackle real-world issues by bringing together researchers, graduate students and partners from different disciplines. Currently, environmental scientists, lawyers and educators at York are researching the application of sustainability principles and practices throughout society. This commitment will leave Canada in a better position to deal with environmental challenges as they arise in the future. It is this collaborative approach to creating new knowledge that makes York a leading research innovator. To learn more about the interdisciplinary university, visit **YORKU.CA**

YORK U
UNIVERSITÉ
UNIVERSITY

redefine THE POSSIBLE.

HUMBER

polytechnic

CHALLENGER QUESTION

Use the following information to answer the next question.

Living in space means living in microgravity. Microgravity is the condition in which gravitational forces acting on the mass of a body are reduced. In a report for science class, Jean-Luc made the following statements regarding the effects of microgravity.

I.   Low gravity makes heart tissue, bones, and muscles grow larger over time.

II. Without gravity, the heart has to do less pumping work, so the heart rate slows down.

III. Mechanisms inside the inner ear that are sensitive to pressure become unbalanced, resulting in disorientation.

IV. Since there is nothing to pull bodily fluids down, fluids migrate from the legs to the head, resulting in congested sinuses.

13. Which of Jean-Luc's statements about the effects of microgravity is **incorrect**?

   A. I   **B.** II   **C.** III   **D.** IV

CHALLENGER QUESTION

14. Microgravity affects all of the following bodily processes **except**

   A. heart rate

   B. skin growth

   C. bone density

   D. muscle retention

9.3.2.1a *through investigations and applications of basic concepts: - identify problems and issues that scientists face when investigating celestial objects and describe ways these problems can be solved*

PROBLEMS IN INVESTIGATIONS

Humans have been observing the night sky from the earliest days, but only recently have there been tools of sufficient quality to allow scientists to look beyond stars that can be seen with the naked eye. The biggest problem with the observation of celestial objects is the huge distances involved. Even intense stars that are larger than our own sun become invisible to us if the star is far enough away. Solutions to this problem require the application of technology to overcome the issue of distance.

Early scientists found that lenses ground into convex shapes could bend light. By arranging these lenses, the magnification of objects could be achieved.

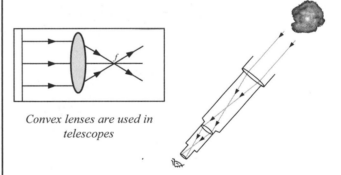

Convex lenses are used in telescopes

The resulting instruments are called telescopes, and they permit astronomers to see objects that are either too distant or too faint to be seen from Earth.

Another issue that telescope users found was that they were constantly having to collect light from distant objects after the light had passed through Earth's atmosphere. The gases and dust in the atmosphere cause images of stars to be slightly blurred.

How could this problem be solved?
One method is to reduce the amount of atmosphere above the observer. Building telescopes on mountaintops achieves this goal.

A mountaintop observatory

Another approach would be to move outside Earth's atmosphere entirely. With space travel and the ability to place satellites in orbit, a telescope can now stay outside the atmosphere and send images back to Earth from space.

Practice

Use the following information to answer the next question.

The Hubble Space Telescope

15. The images received by the Hubble Space Telescope are far superior to the images received by telescopes on Earth because the Hubble Space Telescope

   A. works with lenses that are extremely large

   B. is closer to celestial bodies than telescopes on Earth are

   C. is not affected by pollution and weather present on Earth

   D. works with telescopes on Earth to magnify the images it receives

9.3.2.1b *formulate scientific questions about a problem or issue in space exploration*

SCIENTIFIC QUESTIONS

In order to solve problems that arise in space exploration, specific questions need to be asked to guide the work of scientists. The questions are designed to narrow a larger problem down into smaller, more solvable parts.

:Example

How will people travel to and survive on Mars?

This very general question does not identify any specific problems to be solved. It is too general, and it could not be used to direct the activities of scientists to help solve it.

:Example

For people to survive on Mars, they will have to live in an atmosphere that is 95% carbon dioxide. What can be done to supply enough oxygen for people to breathe?

At first take, the question seems simple enough. If enough oxygen can be supplied to an astronaut in a space suit, then that person can breathe. A person living on Mars, however, probably would not be able to spend all of their time in a space suit. Some form of shelter would have to be provided. Inside this shelter, all of the conditions for a normal existence would have to be supplied. Someone attempting to solve this problem can now identify all of the characteristics of a shelter needed to keep a human being alive. This includes not only oxygen, but light, heat, sufficient air pressure, and protection from the Martian environment.

Robots can explore and work on Mars

Another investigator might look at this question from the point of view of trying to find enough oxygen on Mars for humans to use. It would be impossible for travellers to Mars to bring along enough oxygen for a lengthy stay. Previous investigations of Mars have revealed that the surface is coated in rust, or iron oxide. Oxygen is chemically bonded with iron and is lying around in vast quantities on the surface of Mars. Further investigations would need to be conducted to determine if the surface dust can be mined by a robot. Other questions would ask whether the oxygen could be removed from the iron oxide. The results of these investigations would tell scientists whether or not this approach would provide a good solution to the problem.

Sometimes, asking one question leads to many others that also need to be answered. By exploring issues in this way, scientists can identify problems, identify specific questions that need to be answered, and come up with solutions from those answers once they are found.

9.3.2.1c *demonstrate the skills required to plan and conduct an inquiry about space exploration, using instruments, tools, and apparatus safely, accurately, and effectively*

INQUIRY IN SPACE EXPLORATION

One of the central questions people have about outer space relates to how far away objects really are and how scientists know how far away they are. Mathematics supplies the answer.

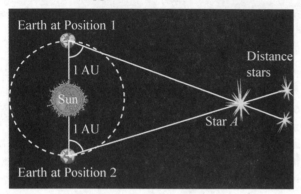

The distance to the distant star is unknown, but the star is visible from Earth at two different positions of Earth relative to the sun. The distance to the sun is known and is generally represented as 1 AU, or astronomical unit. This measure of distance is often used to describe very large distances in space.

The base of the triangle shown is 2 AU across. But, a perpendicular line drawn from the sun to the distant star would create two identical right triangles. Using only one of these triangles, and knowing that 1 AU equals 150 million kilometres, it will be possible to calculate the distance to the star if one more measurement is provided. With the Earth in the position shown, a measurement of the angle to the star is also needed.

SAMPLE CALCULATION

Select a distant object in a schoolyard or park and see if you can calculate the distance to the object. Make sure the space around the object is relatively flat and that you have enough room to move to either side of a central point from which you are viewing the object.

Devise a procedure to collect the data you will need to make the calculation. Before going out to make observations, ensure that you have all the equipment you are going to need.

Gather data and make the calculations. One suggestion is that you gather data for both triangles. In other words, take one angle reading by moving a set distance to the right of your central point, and repeat the process by moving an equal distance to the left and measuring the angle from there.

If possible, check the accuracy of your calculation by asking yourself if your answer makes sense. In other words, is it a reasonable number? If not, then look for mistakes in your calculation. If there is enough time, check the accuracy of your original observations. Try calculating the distance using both of your measurement-data sets, one from the right of the central point and the other from the left. Compare the two results.

Double check, if possible, the accuracy of your answers by physically measuring the distance to the object using a large measuring tape or a laser range finder, if available. Compare this result to your calculated answer.

Use the following information to answer the next question.

Scientists use a spectrograph to identify the primary chemical composition of a star they are studying. They know that certain elements will make different spectral images as shown.

The scientists discover that the star they are studying produces the spectral image shown here

16. The star is **best** described as being composed of

 A. hydrogen and sodium

 B. hydrogen and helium

 C. hydrogen

 D. helium

9.3.2.1d *select and integrate information from various sources, including electronic and print resources, community resources, and personally collected data, to answer the questions chosen*

INFORMATION SOURCES

Research in science requires using different sources that will provide accurate information about the topic you are studying. Information can be from books, from the Internet, or by asking experts in the field. More recent information can also be found in newspaper articles, periodicals, and brochures from government and business agencies.

:Example

Halma has noticed that the phases of the moon always occur in a characteristic way. She notices that the new moon (the moon appears dark against the night sky) is always illuminated from the right side, and that as the phases progress, the illumination of the moon increases from right to left. She is curious about why the moon phases happen in this pattern and decides to investigate.

First quarter moon

Halma has already taken the first step. By observing the pattern of the phases of the moon for herself, she has collected data that she can use to help her understand the reasons for the pattern. She decides to visit the local science centre to see if they can help. The science centre has an observatory that is open for public viewing on the weekends.

9.3.2.1e *organize, record, and analyze the information gathered*

INFORMATION ANALYSIS

Doing scientific research requires that information be collected and recorded. The recorded data is then studied and analyzed. Finally, the data is organized in such a way that a conclusion is made. Consider the following example.

Example

A research project requires students to obtain data on the size (diameter), distance from the sun, and length of year for the first four planets from the sun. Students are asked to analyze the data to look for any relationships that can be found.

How should the students approach this activity?

Step 1: Students need to use various sources to obtain data for each planet.

Step 2: Students should organize data into chart form.

Planet	Distance from Sun (AU)	Diameter of Planet (km)	Period of Orbital Revolution (days)
Mercury	0.39	4 878	88
Venus	0.72	12 104	225
Earth	1	12 756	365.25
Mars	1.52	6 794	687

Step 3: Students could graph the data to help them see trends. Decisions need to be made as to how the graphs should be constructed. Basically, students need to decide which features of the planets they are going to compare. One way of doing it would be to see if there is a relationship amongst that data that depends on how far a planet is from the sun. This could be accomplished by using the data to construct two graphs.

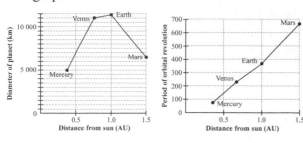

From these graphs, it is possible to see the interrelationships of the data. Students could reach the following conclusions:

- The farther the distance from the sun, the longer the period of orbital revolution for a planet.

It is not possible to identify a relationship between distance from the sun and planet size. If the data set stopped at Earth and did not include Mars, the graph would show a trendline that could lead a student to conclude that the size of the planet increases with distance from the sun. The inclusion of Mars ruins that conclusion. The only thing that can be concluded from the data as it exists is that there is no relationship between planet size and distance from the sun. When seeking relationships in data, it is just as valuable to be able to find a relationship as it is to recognize that no relationship exists.

9.3.2.1f *communicate scientific ideas, procedures, results, and conclusions using appropriate SI units, language, and formats*

COMMUNICATING SCIENTIFIC IDEAS

Many situations in science occur where there is a need to communicate information. Information about distances in space can be communicated using appropriate SI units or other language.

In the metric system, the unit of length or distance is the metre (m). Metres are useful units to describe the length of a car, or the dimensions of a house. When greater distances are involved, they are often measured in kilometres. This unit is equal to 1 000 m and is used to express distances between cities, distances across Canada, or even the diameter of Earth itself.

In space, kilometres are sometimes mentioned, simply because the unit is familiar and it is possible for students to visualize the distances involved, big though they may be. It is possible to talk about the distance from Earth to the sun as being approximately 150 million km. Astronomers find that expressing the distance this way, is also useful to them as they can visualize how far that distance is when comparing it to other distances. In order to simplify the discussion, astronomers usually refer to this distance as 1 AU, or astronomical unit. The AU is an exact distance and is defined as 149 597 870 691 ± 30 m. This is very close to 150 000 000 km, so in common use, the approximation is also given.

USE OF AU IN THE SOLAR SYSTEM

Jupiter is 5.2 AU from the sun. This information tells us the following:

- Jupiter is farther away from the sun than Earth is, since the AU number is greater than 1.
- Jupiter is more than five times farther from the sun than Earth is.

In space beyond our solar system, however, the distances between objects become very large. Scientists have adopted another unit to express these very great distances. It is the light year, or the distance that light travels in one year. Light travels very quickly—nearly 300 000 km/s, so the distance light can travel in one year is an enormous distance. One light year is equal to 9 460 730 472 580.8 km. That is also the same as 63 241 AU.

USE OF LIGHT YEARS IN THE UNIVERSE

Alpha Centauri is the closest star to Earth besides the sun itself. The distance to Alpha Centauri is 4.4 ly (light years, sometimes written as lya, or light years away). Rigel is a very bright star and is a part of the constellation Orion. It is approximately 773 ly from Earth.

- When you look at Alpha Centauri, you are seeing what the star looked like 4.4 years ago. That is how long it took for the light from the star to reach Earth.
- Alpha Centauri is the third brightest star in the sky. Rigel is the sixth brightest. How is it possible for a star that is so far away to be so bright? Research the features of Rigel to discover how this can happen.

9.3.2.2 *conduct investigations on the motion of visible celestial objects, using instruments, tools, and apparatus safely, accurately, and effectively*

CONDUCTING INVESTIGATIONS ON THE MOTION OF THE SUN

Many students tend to think of the motion of the sun in the sky as simply rising in the east and setting in the west. By actually conducting investigations and collecting data on the motion of the sun, a new understanding can be reached about how Earth moves around the sun.

To do this effectively, students need to set up the necessary equipment, arrange schedules for collecting data throughout the day and over time, and build appropriate data tables.

SUN OBSERVATION EQUIPMENT

It is extremely important that students realize that they can never look directly at the sun, even for an instant. Light from the sun is extremely powerful and can cause blindness, or very permanent and painful damage to eyes. Therefore, it is vital that observations of the position of the sun be taken by looking at the shadows the sun casts. Safe instruments can be used to provide the following sorts of information:

- position of the sun on the horizon at sunrise and sunset
- angle of the sun from the horizon at points throughout the day
- time of sunrise and sunset

Collecting data and graphing the results will provide representations of what happens to the position of the sun at different times of the year. It is therefore important to collect information throughout a school year to get a sense of what happens over time.

INTERPRETING THE INFORMATION

The information collected might surprise some students, and the patterns in the data need to be interpreted. The first thing that students need to think about is the fact that Earth is tilted on its axis by 23.5 degrees.

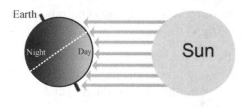

Earth is tilted relative to its orbit around the sun.

This tilt is maintained throughout the orbit of Earth. This results in the North Pole pointing away from the sun at one time of the year and toward the sun at another.

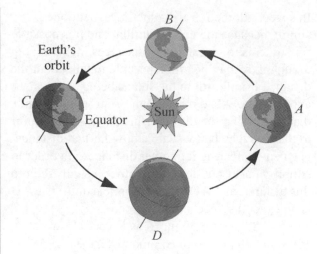

Position of Earth at different times of the year.

Analysis of the data can be helped along by considering some guiding questions.

- At which position of Earth is North America experiencing winter?
- What causes the seasons?
- During which season is the sun angle from the horizon at its lowest?
- Does the sun angle ever reach directly overhead? Is there a place on Earth where it could be directly overhead?
- Days are shorter in the winter than they are in the summer. Does your data support this statement?
- When the sun rises, does it always rise in the same location? Explain by studying the position of Earth at different times of the year.

Practice

17. Which of the following statements describes how optical telescopes assess conditions beyond Earth?

   A. They detect radio waves emitted by distant stars.

   B. They conduct electromagnetic radiation from the sun.

   C. They magnify distant celestial objects by using lenses and mirrors.

   D. They detect the chemical composition of the atmosphere of distant stars.

9.3.2.3 *gather, organize, and record data through regular observations of the night sky and/or use of appropriate software programs, and use these data to identify and study the motion of visible celestial objects*

OBSERVATIONS OF THE NIGHT SKY

Many people have come to recognize some of the most common constellations in the night sky.

Four constellations: Orion (centre), and clockwise left to right, Taurus, Canis Major, and Canis Minor

Constellations will move over the course of an evening. This is because Earth is rotating underneath our feet, and if we remain standing in one spot, then the relative positions of the stars will change. To demonstrate this, use a star chart to locate the Big Dipper. It will be found in the north sky and should be high in the sky at all times.

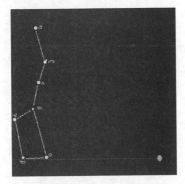

The Big Dipper (left) and Polaris (right).

Polaris can be located by imagining a straight line through the two stars that make up the far edge of the ladle. Extend the line out about five times the distance between the two stars.

PROCEDURE

Stand in one spot and locate the Big Dipper and Polaris. Make a diagram of the main stars that are visible. It could look something like this:

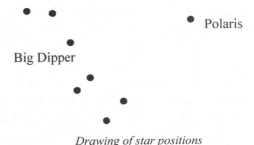

Drawing of star positions

Make note of the time that the observations were made. Return to the same spot and look in the same direction two or three hours later. Repeat the drawing. Be careful to draw the star positions as they appear in the sky. Compare the two diagrams.

If you were able to observe the positions of the Big Dipper and Polaris over the course of 24 hours, the drawings you would make would look like the following.

One observation might be made-Polaris did not change it's position. Standing in one spot and looking at Polaris, all the other stars have moved around it. This is because Polaris is the only star in the Northern Hemisphere that has the axis of Earth pointing directly at it. Sometimes, Polaris is called the North Star because the direction someone faces when looking at the star is always north.

9.3.3.1 *identify and assess the impact of developments in space research and technology on other fields of endeavour*

DEVELOPMENTS IN SPACE RESEARCH AND TECHNOLOGY

The International Space Station (ISS), the Hubble telescope, the Mars Rovers, and space probes that are moving toward the outer regions of our solar system are all examples of technology developed for travel and life in space. Scientists asked questions and conducted research to develop these new technologies. Many of these new technologies found a new home on Earth. New developments in space technology have had a large impact in other fields like robotics, navigation, telecommunications and resource management.

NAVIGATION AND TELECOMMUNICATION

Many satellites orbit the Earth and serve many different purposes. Some may monitor weather, others bounce back television and radio signals. Some satellites send back detailed information about the surface of the Earth that has helped developed newer and more accurate maps. This has allowed the commercial use of GPS, or global positioning systems in vehicles like cars, boats, and planes. GPS devices are now available to purchase and are used for a variety of purposes, from surveying to travel navigation, by a wide range of people. Many are easy to use and make life on Earth easier using technology developed for space. Newer, more advanced weather satellites can now be used to track developing storms and provide information to the public about any dangers they might pose. Satellites are also being used to track sea ice levels in the Arctic and Antarctica and to monitor global temperatures, providing scientists with important information about climate change.

The GOES-9 Weather Satellite picture of hurricane Felix

New developments in satellite technologies have also helped improve telecommunication on Earth. High quality television signals, satellite phone signals, and radio signals all make use of satellite technology in providing services to people in everyday life.

RESOURCE MANAGEMENT

Travelling and living in space requires specific technologies that allow humans to survive. In particular, scientists first had to figure out ways to meet the astronauts physical needs while in space. This led to the development of technologies that can recycle water and oxygen continuously so that large amounts are not needed on missions, leaving more room on rockets, shuttles and the International Space Station. These new technologies also helped in resource management on Earth. Increased abilities to recycle materials, like water, help ensure clean water for drinking and also that water is cleaned and returned to the environment after if has been used in houses or even industrial factories.

ROBOTICS

The development of new technologies for space exploration has had a large impact on the field of robotics. The Mars Rovers are able to move about on the surface of Mars and dig, collect, and analyze samples of soil and rocks. The most recent Mars Lander, the Phoenix, has a thermal and evolved gas analyzer on board that uses eight ovens to test samples of soil and ice. It is also equipped with robotic arms and cameras, as well as a meteorological station to analyze the surface weather conditions of the planet.

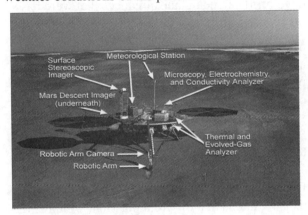

The Phoenix Mars Lander

The advancement of new robotic technologies can also help in areas other than space exploration. Robotic arms are now able to perform very delicate surgeries on patients and can be operated by doctors using controls thousands of kilometres away. Technology from space shuttle fuel pumps was used in developing better artificial hearts for humans who need them to live.

New robotic systems also allow scientists to see farther into space than ever before. The Hubble Space Telescope was designed to operate from orbit, allowing it to view space without worrying about environmental conditions on Earth like pollution or bad weather. It has sent back clear images of far regions of space and has helped scientists gain a better understanding of the universe.

*The Hubble
Space Telescope*

OTHER AREAS

Space research has led to spin-off technologies in other areas, as well. Flame-resistant suits were first developed for space exploration. Technology to improve the traction of tires was developed from advanced parachute material from the Viking space mission.

As new space technologies continue to be developed, they are also put to practical uses on Earth.

Practice

18. Robotic systems and the development of wireless communications are space technologies that have been used on Earth to develop
   A. digital imaging
   B. improved safety helmets
   C. microlaser communications
   D. voice-controlled wheelchairs

9.3.3.2 *relate the beliefs of various cultures concerning celestial objects to aspects of their civilization*

CULTURE AND CELESTIAL OBJECTS

Common throughout history are stories based on groups of stars in the sky called constellations. The ancient Greeks fashioned myths about the constellations that are still told today.

Constellations

The ancient Greeks named the constellations and planets after legendary figures, animals, or gods. Orion the hunter is one of the better known constellations in the sky. Greek legend states that Diana, the goddess of the moon and hunting, fell in love with Orion, the bravest hunter of ancient times. According to the myth, Diana drove a moon chariot across the sky at night. She began to neglect these duties in order to help Orion with his hunting on Earth. When Diana's brother Apollo heard this, he decided to trick Diana into accidentally killing Orion from far away. After this occurred, Diana put Orion's body into the darkest part of the sky, and the sky became bright with stars that outlined his body. The constellation consists of seven major stars, two that form his shoulders and feet and three that form his belt.

Stars and constellations have been used for thousands of years for navigation across land and over oceans before the invention of the compass.

Other cultures learned how to predict the movements of the planets and stars and recorded celestial events. The Maya civilization used celestial events to mark religious occasions and to develop calendars to keep track of time. The Maya people were keen astronomers and had mapped out the phases of celestial objects, especially the moon and sun. Many of their temples have doorways and other features aligning to celestial events. They also developed calendars and almanacs that were based on celestial objects.

Many First Nations cultures developed art, architecture, and histories that wove the stars and planets into their daily lives. Stories relating to constellations helped explain their positions in the sky. The Iroquois called the Big Dipper the Great Bear. Three stars in the constellation were thought to be hunters chasing the bear, one with a weapon, one with a pot for cooking, and the last with firewood. By the time the Big Dipper moved across the sky, it was in a different position, which symbolized the success of the hunters. Some other groups, however, believed that the three stars were cubs following the mother bear.

There are also stories that deal with other objects in the solar system, like the moon. According to such stories, the moon was created so that people could see during the night.

Space and the stars have been studied for many generations and by many different cultures. They have inspired many different stories, traditions, and theories.

Use the following information to answer the next question.

The constellation Great Bear consists of seven bright stars. It is visible throughout the year in the Northern Hemisphere. An illustration of the constellation is shown here.

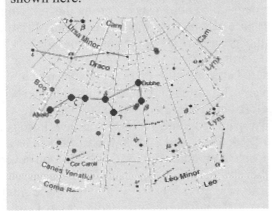

19. The constellation Great Bear is also known as

A. Orion

B. Draco

C. Leo Minor

D. Ursa Major

Use the following information to answer the next question.

Classical Greek mythology created stories to explain constellations in space. One such constellation is shown here.

Constellations have been named according to their formations.

20. Which constellation is shown in the above figure?

A. Canis Minor (Little Dog)

B. Great Bear

C. Hercules

D. Orion

9.3.3.3 *provide examples of the contributions of Canadian research and development to space exploration and technology*

- Canadarm—Also known as the Shuttle Remote Manipulator System, the Canadarm is a well-known Canadian invention and is used on all the space shuttles. It was designed and built by the National Research Council and several Canadian companies. The Canadarm acts like a human arm and has shoulder, elbow, and wrist joints, which are held together with upper and lower arm booms. It is 15.2 metres long, and weighs about 410 kilograms on Earth. It is used to grab and move heavy objects, support objects in need of repair, and support astronauts during space walks. It has special sensors and cameras to find damage to equipment and the space shuttle.
- Canada's most recent addition to space exploration is a new tool that will work in conjunction with the Canadarm aboard the International Space Station. This tool is called Dextre. Dextre's moving parts resemble the fingers of a hand that is attached to an arm. It will perform tasks that astronauts usually carry out, as well as other jobs that require very precise movements.

The Canadarm with Dextre

- The Microvariability and Oscillations of Stars telescope (MOST)—Canada's first space telescope. It is sometimes called the "Humble" space telescope. It is the smallest space telescope yet made and sits in a satellite about the size of a suitcase. MOST is designed to study stars to find out their age, behaviour, and composition, and it also examines stars that have planets orbiting them. MOST can focus on a star for up to seven weeks in a row, which provides astronomers with more details about a star. Putting this telescope in space also helps avoid the distortion of Earth's atmosphere that is seen through telescopes on Earth.
- Marc Garneau—the first Canadian astronaut in space. He started his career in the Canadian Navy before being accepted into the Canadian Astronaut Program. He made journeys into space in 1984, 1996, and 2000 and also worked as a capsule communicator, or CAPCOM, on several other space missions. A CAPCOM is a person on Earth who gives messages from the space shuttle crew to the mission control centre. Marc Garneau was also president of the Canadian Space Agency from 2001 to 2005.
- Roberta Bondar—in 1992, she became the first Canadian female astronaut to go into space. She is a neurologist and holds several degrees. Dr. Bondar worked for NASA for 10 years as head of space medicine. She and her team studied how space flight affects the human body, and how the body recovers from being in space. This knowledge has helped doctors learn more about diseases on Earth. She now works as a speaker and consultant for businesses, scientists, and medical communities. She is also a writer and nature photographer, and has published several books.

Marc Garneau (left) and Roberta Bondar (right) are two of Canada's astronauts.

- Richard Bond—astronomer, university professor, and director of the Canadian Institute for Theoretical Astrophysics (CITA). Bond's research explores how the universe was created, what size it is, and how old it is. To do this, he studies light and sound energy, that may have been made at the time the universe formed. Dr. Bond's work has helped scientists discover what the universe looks like. His work has helped scientists learn that the universe is flat and that it is expanding. It also supports the idea that some form of energy is causing the universe to expand. This energy is called dark energy. It is stronger than the force of gravity. Many scientists believe that it makes up most of the universe's mass and energy.

- David Levy—astronomer and science writer. He has discovered more than 22 comets, as well as other space objects. He co-discovered the comet Shoemaker-Levy 9, which collided with Jupiter in 1994. This comet was captured by Jupiter's gravity, causing it to break apart. The pieces hit the surface of the planet, causing great fireballs to erupt. Dark marks were left behind.

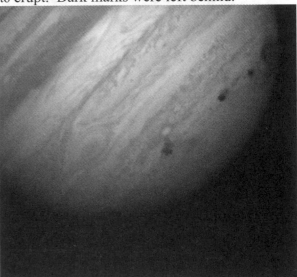

The dark marks show where parts of comet Shoemaker-Levy 9 impacted on the surface of Jupiter.

Helen Hogg—astronomer and university professor. Much of her work involved studying globular clusters. A globular cluster is a mass of stars bound together by gravity. There are 150 known globular clusters in the Milky Way. She taught astronomy at the University of Toronto and encouraged people, especially women, to study the stars and be interested in science. She died in 1993, but her contributions to astronomy will be remembered for years to come.

Practice

21. Which of the following eminent Canadian personalities is known for her research on the distinctive stars in globular clusters?

    A. Helen Hogg

    B. Annie Cannon

    C. Roberta Bondar

    D. Bjarni Tryggvason

Use the following information to answer the next question.

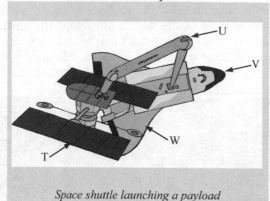

Space shuttle launching a payload

22. Canadian scientists are recognized for their part in the Space Shuttle Program because they designed the structure labelled

A. *U* **B.** *T* **C.** *W* **D.** *V*

9.3.3.4 *explore careers in science and technology that are related to the exploration of space, and identify their educational requirements*

CAREERS IN SPACE EXPLORATION
ENGINEERS

There are many different areas of engineering that are involved in space exploration, such as mechanical engineering and electrical engineering. Engineers can design and build technology for use in space exploration. Engineers rely on a strong understanding of physics and math. Engineering degrees deal mostly with these subjects and specialized areas related to the particular engineering area a person chooses. People with strong math and physics skills generally have the requirements to enter the field of engineering. Engineering deals with many of the aspects involved in space exploration, such as shuttle technology, robotics, clothing and spacecraft design, and satellites. Specialization in particular areas usually helps engineers gain a better understanding of one specific field.

ASTRONOMERS

Astronomy deals with the classification and position of objects and phenomenon in space. Scientists explain such phenomenon using astrophysics. Many astronomers are highly educated, have degrees in astronomy or physics, and are employed by private organizations or universities to conduct research. Many have been trained in the use of sophisticated telescopes and technology needed to study phenomenon in space and know how analyze the information received by such tools. However, many people study astronomy on their own as amateur astronomers in communities all over the world using smaller telescopes.

MEDICINE

As humans continue to travel to space, scientists continue to develop new medicines and treatments to help them. To study the physical effects of the space environment on humans, scientists usually need an education in medicine. Training in this area usually involves gaining advanced knowledge of biology, and, in particular, human biology. Careers in medicine require extensive schooling at the university level and are competitive to enter into. Many scientists in the field of medicine need training for using laboratory equipment and medical technologies that test and assess patients' conditions.

New research in zero-gravity environments can help to develop treatments for medical conditions on Earth as well as new technologies to help diagnose and treat patients.

Practice

Use the following information to answer the next question.

Kyle wants to research and design new technologies used in space exploration. He is looking ahead to figure out what type of education he needs to reach his goal.

23. Which of the following subjects will Kyle **most likely** need to study in order to research and design new technologies in space exploration?

A. Astrology **B.** Astronomy

C. Engineering **D.** Biochemistry

Use the following information to answer the next question.

There are many different disciplines associated with researching and carrying out space exploration. Each requires a specific set of skills and knowledge. For instance, a scientist may want to study the effects of prolonged exposure to microgravity on humans in space.

24. A scientist who wishes to study the effects of prolonged exposure to microgravity on humans would **most likely** need an educational background in?

A. Physics

B. Medicine

C. Chemistry

D. Engineering

SOLUTIONS–EARTH AND SPACE SCIENCE: SPACE EXPLORATION

1. OR	6. A	11. A	16. B	21. A
2. D	7. OR	12. B	17. C	22. A
3. B	8. A	13. A	18. D	23. C
4. OR	9. D	14. B	19. D	24. B
5. B	10. OR	15. C	20. D	

1. Open Response

Points	Sample Answer
4	4 points total: any statements that include the following: • The numbers are very big. • Distances are easier to understand when the numbers are rounded off and not exact. • The huge distances between objects can be very hard to measure exactly. • It would take too long to take an exact measurement.

2. D

The Milky Way galaxy consists of several spiral arms. The four major spiral arms of the Milky Way are the Perseus arm, the Norma and Cygnus arm, the Crux and Scutum arm, and the Carina and Sagittarius arm. A small spiral arm known as the Orion arm exists between the Perseus arm and the Carina and Sagittarius arm. Our solar system lies at the inner rim of the Orion arm. In the given figure, point S represents the position of our solar system in the Milky Way galaxy.

3. B

One light year is equal to 9.46×10^{12} km, and one astronomical unit is equal to 150 million km.
The correct answer is D.

4. Open Response

As a result of increasing distances between stars, the wavelengths of light travelling from the stars toward Earth shift toward the higher wavelength, which is red light. If a star is showing this redshift, it indicates it is travelling away from Earth. Many stars show this, indicating that the universe is expanding.

5. B

The big bang theory states that the universe began approximately 13 to 14 billion years ago with a massive explosion that led to a hot and dense state called the primordial condition. The celestial bodies in the universe are still moving away from each other, which supports the idea that the universe is still expanding. This evidence of the expanding universe supports the big bang theory.

6. A

According to the Big Bang theory, a massive explosion occurred in space about 15 billion years ago, beginning a reaction that created to the universe.

7. Open Response

Tides are caused by the pull of the force of gravity of the moon and the sun on Earth. Water on Earth is visibly affected, as it is a liquid and is free to move in response to this force. Oceans can actually rise and fall depending on the positions of the sun and the moon. If the sun and the moon are in line with each other (as shown in the given illustration), the effects of gravity are the greatest. Tides will be at their highest in areas on the surface of Earth that are pointing at the sun or the moon. If water were to move toward these regions of Earth, then it stands to reason that the water will leave other areas that are not pointing toward the sun and moon. These areas will experience a low tide.

Since Earth rotates completely once a day, one location on Earth will experience two high tides and two low tides in a 24-hour period.

8. A

For all the planets but Venus, it seems that the slower the rotation of the planet, the faster its orbital revolution around the sun is. However, when Venus is taken into account, there appears to be no connection between the rotation of the planet to its revolution around the sun.

For example, Mercury rotates on its axis every 59 days and revolves around the sun every 88 days.

Earth, which is farther from the sun, rotates on its axis much quicker (every 24 hours) and revolves around the sun slower (every 365 days).

Venus, which is farther from the sun than Mercury but closer than Earth, rotates much slower than either Mercury or Earth (243 days). However, while Venus revolves around the sun much faster than Earth, it does not revolve the sun faster than Mercury, which it should for the pattern to hold true.

9. D

Alternative D is the correct response.

This region is known as the Oort cloud. Although no direct observation of the Oort cloud has been made, indirect evidence hints that it consists of millions of comet nuclei. This gives some support to the hypothesis that this area is the source of long-period comets.

10. Open Response

Solar winds carry charged particles into Earth's atmosphere. These particles collide with Earth's magnetosphere (the atmosphere above the magnetic North Pole) to produce electromagnetic radiation that is visible in different colours. During peak solar activity, aurora borealis can be seen in the southern part of Canada and the northern United States.

11. A

The electromagnetic spectrum is the frequency range of all possible electromagnetic radiation. It is arranged in increasing order of wavelength and includes gamma rays, X-rays, ultraviolet rays, visible light, infrared rays, microwaves, radio waves, and long waves.

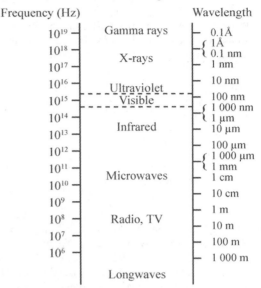

In the electromagnetic spectrum, visible light lies between ultraviolet and infrared rays.

The correct answer is A.

12. B

A continuous stream of charged particles flowing out from the sun's surface into the whole of the solar system is called the solar wind. The solar wind contains many harmful rays that also affect Earth. Earth's atmosphere functions to shield the planet from this radiation, protecting organisms from its damaging effects.

13. A

Jean-Luc's incorrect statement is that low gravity makes heart tissue, bones, and muscles grow larger over time. The other three statements do describe the results of being in a microgravity environment.

14. B

Microgravity affects all of the bodily processes shown except skin growth

15. C

Because the Hubble Space Telescope is in orbit, it is not affected by pollution or weather on Earth.

16. B

Comparing the spectrograph readings to the spectral images of the three elements shown, the star is primarily made up of hydrogen and helium.

17. C

Optical telescopes magnify images of distant celestial objects using lenses and mirrors. This helps astronomers to have a clearer look at celestial objects to assess their conditions and compositions.

18. D

Robotic systems and advanced communications are space technologies that have been used on Earth for the development of voice-controlled wheelchairs.

19. D

The constellation Great Bear is also referred to by its Latin name, *Ursa Major*.

20. D

Orion is the name of the constellation whose formation resembles the hunter.

21. A

Helen Hogg was among the first female astronomers in Canada. She extensively researched new areas of space, particularly the stars in globular clusters. Helen Hogg wrote over 200 academic papers in her lifetime. Her work not only carved out a place for women in Canadian scientific academia, but it also contributed significantly to the body of knowledge available to astronomers.

22. A

Canadians designed the structure known as the Canadarm, indicated by U.

23. C

Kyle will most likely need to study engineering in university. Engineering will provide him with the education he needs to do research into the development of new technologies. Studying engineering will provide him with both the theoretical and practical knowledge about mechanical and electrical systems.

24. B

A scientist who wishes to study the effects of microgravity on humans in space would most likely need to have an educational background in medicine. Scientists dealing with this subject would need to know all the physical conditions associated with space travel and their physical effects in order to research new ways of helping astronauts treat such conditions.

1. Which of the following units of measurement is **most suitable** for measuring the distance between two galaxies?

    A. Miles   B. Kilometres

    C. Light years   D. Light minutes

2. Which of the following graphs correctly represents the relative sizes of the sun, Earth, the solar system, and the Milky Way?

    A.

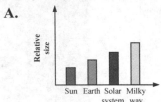

    B.

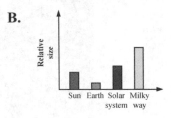

    C.

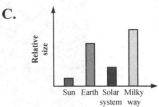

    D.

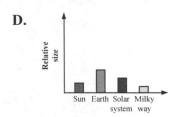

CHALLENGER QUESTION

Use the following information to answer the next question.

In 1610, Galileo Galilei observed moons orbiting the planet Jupiter. This went directly against the theory that the Earth was the centre of the universe and led to a new scientific theory on the design of the universe. It has now been proven that all of the planets in our solar system orbit the sun and several planets have their own moons.

3. Which of the following statements **best** describes the logical reasoning that led to the development of the new model of our solar system?

    A. If moons orbit other planets, these planets can still revolve around Earth.

    B. If there are moons orbiting Jupiter, then it makes sense that every planet has moons and orbits the sun

    C. If there are moons orbiting Jupiter, then everything in the solar system must revolve around Jupiter

    D. If there are moons orbiting Jupiter, then not every object in space is orbiting the Earth meaning Earth is not at the centre of the solar system.

Use the following information to answer the next question.

The Kuiper belt is a region in the solar system made of a large collection of small spatial bodies mainly composed of ice, frozen methane, and frozen ammonia.

4. Where is the Kuiper belt located?
   A. Within the orbit of Mercury

   B. Beyond the orbit of Neptune

   C. Between the orbits of Jupiter and Mars

   D. Between the orbits of Saturn and Neptune

Use the following information to answer the next question.

The planets of our solar system are divided into two groups. The inner planets of Mercury, Venus, Earth, and Mars are called terrestrial planets. The outer planets of Jupiter, Saturn, Neptune, and Uranus are called Jovian planets.

5. The reason the outer planets are called Jovian planets is that they
   A. are far away from the sun and have low temperatures

   B. have equal rotation and revolution periods

   C. are of the same size and composition

   D. are large and gaseous

6. The sun radiates energy in the form of
   A. solar wind

   B. wind energy

   C. nuclear energy

   D. electromagnetic waves

Use the following information to answer the next question.

Four effects of living in space
I.   Must cope with crowded conditions
II. Bones become less dense
III. Danger of malfunctioning equipment
IV. Spinal column stretches

7. Astronauts living in a space environment must cope with biological and psychological effects. Which of the above pairs of factors are both classified as psychological effects?
   A. II and III   B. II and IV

   C. I and IV   D. I and III

8. Which of the following statements explains how the issue of limited water supply is dealt with on a spacecraft?
   A. Water is reused several times before being discarded.

   B. Ice is collected from outside the spacecraft.

   C. Stored ice is melted into water.

   D. Water is recycled continually.

9. Which of the following methods of viewing the sun through a telescope is **most advisable**?
   A. Wear sunglasses while looking through the eyepiece.

   B. Keep the eyes a distance of at least 15 cm from the eyepiece.

   C. Focus on the vicinity of the sun but not right at it and look at the area around the sun.

   D. Hold a white card about 15 cm behind the eyepiece and look at the image produced.

10. A spectrograph is an instrument that

    A. is used to study life forms on other planets

    B. studies the gaseous constituents of other planets

    C. senses gamma rays emitted by other objects in space

    D. is used to photograph a spectrum from other sources in space

Open Response

Use the following information to answer the next question.

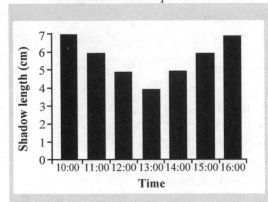

Daryl made the following graph by recording information he collected after observing the shadows cast by a small plant.

11. Describe how the sun's position in the sky, and its location relative to the horizon affected the length of the shadows recorded by Daryl.

_____

_____

_____

_____

_____

_____

_____

12. The technology for the improvement of car tire traction is adapted from space technology that was developed for

    A. advanced parachute material

    B. the structural analysis of spacecrafts

    C. the analysis of rocket engine emissions

    D. the design of microcircuitry for electronics

Open Response

Use the following information to answer the next question.

Research into space technology has had a large impact on technology for use on Earth. In particular, people now have access to updated maps and better satellite navigation tools. One such technology is the global positioning system, more commonly known as GPS.

13. A car is stuck in a remote rural area, but luckily it has a GPS system. Explain what GPS is and how it works to locate the stranded vehicle.

_____

_____

_____

_____

_____

_____

_____

_____

Use the following information to answer the next question.

One of the constellations consists of seven major stars—two forming shoulders, two forming feet, and three forming a belt. This constellation is visible in the Northern Hemisphere in fall and winter.

14. What is the name of the constellation described?

A. Orion **B.** Aries

C. Pisces **D.** Gemini

Use the following information to answer the next question.

Microvariability and Oscillations of Stars Telescope (MOST) is Canada's first space telescope. It sits in a satellite about the size of a suitcase and is the smallest space telescope. MOST is used to study the ages of stars and to search for any planets orbiting them.

15. What is the MOST telescope sometimes called because of its size?

A. Humble space telescope

B. Hubble space telescope

C. Suitcase telescope

D. Skylab telescope

16. Melissa has always been inspired and intrigued by the characteristics and movements of different objects in the solar system. She aspires to have a career that involves studying the solar system and outer space. Melissa wants to become an

A. engineer **B.** architect

C. astrologer **D.** astronomer

SOLUTIONS

1. C	5. D	9. D	13. OR
2. B	6. D	10. D	14. A
3. D	7. D	11. OR	15. A
4. B	8. D	12. A	16. D

1. C

One light year is the distance travelled by light through space in one year. Light years are used to measure very large distances, such as the distance between two stars. In space, light takes years to travel from one galaxy to another galaxy; therefore, light years are the most appropriate unit for measuring the distance between two galaxies.

Distractor Rationale

Miles, kilometres, and light minutes are distance-measuring units. Miles and kilometres are used to measure long distances on Earth's surface. Light minutes measure the distance travelled by light through space in one minute. These units are too small to measure the distance between two galaxies.

2. B

The relative sizes of the sun, Earth, solar system, and Milky Way are correctly represented by the graph in alternative B

Earth is a planet that revolves around the sun. The sun is about 333 000 times larger than Earth. The solar system consists of eight planets that revolve around the sun. The Milky Way is the galaxy that houses the solar system. It consists of about 400 billion stars and their planets.

3. D

Logical reasoning led to the development of the new model of our solar system. Once it was shown that there were moons orbiting Jupiter, it was understood that not every object in space is orbiting the Earth. This proved that the Earth was not the centre of the universe.

It is not logical to assume that every planet has moons just because one other planet has them, and there is no logical connection between every planet having moons and every planet orbiting the sun. It is also not logical to assume that the universe revolves around Jupiter, when our own moon revolves around the Earth. The main evidence against the theory of the Earth being the centre of the universe is that moons orbiting Jupiter cannot also be orbiting the Earth.

4. B

The Kuiper belt is located beyond the orbit of Neptune. Most comets are believed to originate from this region.

5. D

Alternative D is the correct response.

The Jovian planets are all gas giants like Jupiter. The word "Jovian" means Jupiter-like.

6. D

The sun radiates energy in the form of heat and light. It radiates electromagnetic radiation in the region of ultraviolet waves, visible light, and infrared waves.

7. D

Astronauts have to cope with crowded conditions and are aware of the risks related to the dangers of malfunctioning equipment. These are psychological effects, while spinal column stretching and bone density are biological factors.

8. D

Spacecrafts are equipped with machines that enable the water used by astronauts to be recycled continually. This allows the astronauts to survive in space and also prevents the need to store large quantities of water on board for missions.

9. D

You should never look directly at the sun through a telescope. Holding a card about 15 cmfrom the eyepiece will produce an image of the sun that is safe to view.

10. D

A spectroscope is an instrument that can be attached to a telescope to record a photographic image of a spectrum. It is one of the most important tools used by astronomers to study celestial objects.

11. Open Response

The shadow appeared longer in earlier and later times due to the sun's position relative to the horizon. This is due to the movement of Earth. As Earth spins on its axis, the sun's position in the sky changes. At midday, the sun is highest in the sky, or farthest from the horizon. This produces the shortest shadow from people and objects on the surface of Earth. As the sun moves back toward the horizon, the angle as it sets produces longer shadows similar to the length of those in the morning.

12. A

The technology for the improvement of car tire traction is adapted from the space technology that arose from the development of parachute material for the Viking space mission.

Various technologies developed for space exploration are used for technological advancement in various fields on Earth.

13. **Open Response**

GPS, or Global Positioning System, works by sending signals to a satellite. A built-in receiver sends signals to a minimum of three orbiting satellites. From the satellite signals, a computer calculation can pinpoint the exact location of the stranded vehicle.

14. **A**

The description of the constellation is referring to Orion. Constellations are patterns of stars that have been used for centuries to organize the night sky according to the pictures these patterns appear to make. Orion is a distinctive arrangement of stars that brightens the night sky from December to April. According to ancient Greek mythology, Orion was a giant and a great hunter.

15. **A**

MOST is also known as the "Humble" telescope.

16. **D**

Astronomy refers to the study of planets, moons, stars, and galaxies, their nature and their positions. Melissa wants to be an astronomer.

Electrical Applications

Physics: Electrical Applications

Table of Correlations

	Specific Expectation	Practice Questions	Unit Test Questions
9.4.1	Understanding Basic Concepts		
9.4.1.1	*explain common electrostatic phenomena*	1, 2, 3	1
9.4.1.3	*describe the concepts of electric current, potential difference, and resistance, with the help of a water analogy*	7, 8, 9	3
9.4.1.4	*explain how electric current, potential difference, and resistance are measured using an ammeter and a voltmeter*	10, 11	4
9.4.1.5	*describe qualitatively the effects of varying electrical resistance and potential difference on electric current in an electrical circuit;*	12	5
9.4.1.6	*apply the relationship potential difference = resistance × current resistance current to simple series circuits*	13, 14	6, 7
9.4.1.7	*determine quantitatively the percent efficiency of an electrical device that converts electrical energy to other forms of energy, using the relationship percent efficiency = $\dfrac{energy\ output}{energy\ input} \times 100$*	15, 16	8, 9
9.4.1.2	*compare qualitatively static and current electricity*	4, 5, 6	2
9.4.2	Developing Skills of Inquiry and Communication		
9.4.2.1a	*"through investigations and applications of basic concepts:— demonstrate knowledge of electrical safety procedures when planning and carrying out investigations and choosing and using materials, tools, and equipment"*	17	10
9.4.2.1c	*- formulate questions about the problem or issue*		
9.4.2.1d	*- demonstrate the skills required to plan and conduct an inquiry into the use of electricity, using instruments, tools, and apparatus safely, accurately, and effectively*	19	
9.4.2.1e	*- select and integrate information from various sources, including electronic and print resources, community resources, and personally collected data, to answer the questions chosen*		
9.4.2.1f	*- organize, record, and analyse the information gathered*		
9.4.2.1g	*- communicate scientific ideas, procedures, results, and conclusions using appropriate SI units, language, and formats*		
9.4.2.2	*design, draw, and construct series and parallel circuits that perform a specific function*	20	14
9.4.2.3	*use appropriate instruments to collect and graph data, and determine the relationship between voltage and current in a simple series circuit with a single resistor*		
9.4.2.4	*charge an electroscope by contact and by induction*		
9.4.2.1b	*- identify an authentic practical challenge or problem related to the use of electricity*	18	
9.4.3	Relating Science to Technology, Society, and the Environment		
9.4.3.1	*describe and explain household wiring and its typical components*	21	11
9.4.3.3	*compare electrical energy production technologies, including risks and benefits*	23, 24	12
9.4.3.4	*explain how some common household electrical appliances operate*	25, 26	13
9.4.3.5	*describe careers that involve electrical technologies, and use employability assessment programs, newspaper job advertisements, and/or appropriate Internet sources to identify the knowledge and skill requirements of such careers*	27	

Specific Expectation		Practice Questions	Unit Test Questions
9.4.3.2	*develop a solution to a practical problem related to the use of electricity in the home, school, or community*	22	

9.4.1.1 *explain common electrostatic phenomena*

ELECTROSTATIC PHENOMENA

One January morning, Carol had a few encounters with static electricity. First, as she shuffled half awake to open her bedroom door, she received a shock when she touched the doorknob. Next, as she tried to brush her long hair, her hair just kept standing up. Then, when she went to the laundry room to pull clothes out of the dryer, Carol found one of her brother's socks stuck to her favourite sweater. What caused all of the static electricity that Carol kept encountering?

Static electricity passes from a hand to a door knob

CHARGES IN THE ATOM

All matter is made up of small particles called atoms. At the core of the atom is a nucleus composed of neutral charged neutrons and positive charged protons. A cloud of negative charged electrons surrounds the nucleus.

Proton = particle with a positive charge found in the nucleus of the atom

Neutron = particle with a negative charge found in the nucleus of the atom

Electron = tiny particles with a negative charge moving around the nucleus

The overall charge of a substance depends the charges of the atoms in the substance.

- An atom becomes positively charged when electrons are taken away, leaving more positive charges than negative ones in the atom.
- An atom becomes negatively charged when electrons are added, leaving more negative charges than positive ones in the atom.
- An atom is neutral when the positive charges are equal to the negative charges.

STATIC ELECTRICITY

Static electricity is the accumulation and storage of charged particles, resulting in a charged object. However, recall that the proton is held within the nucleus of an atom, and it is very difficult to move because of the forces in the nucleus. If electrons are transferred between objects, they create a charge that can be held in one place. This charge is static electricity, or static charge.

Returning to Carol's encounters with static electricity, the static electricity was the result of moving charges. As Carol shuffled across the floor, electrons transferred to her socks from the carpet. The sock and carpet both have a neutral charge to start. As the sock rubbed along the carpet, electrons transferred to the sock. The sock then had a negative charge and the carpet had a positive charge. Touching something that is neutral or positively charged would result in an electrical discharge in the form of a spark and shock.

As well, when Carol brushed her hair, electrons transferred between the comb and her hair. The more she brushed, the more charges transferred to her hair. Clothing in the dryer will transfer electrons as they tumble, causing the clothes to become charged.

Practice

Use the following information to answer the next question.

After combing her dry hair, Nancy put her comb down on her dressing table near some scraps of paper. She observed that the scraps of paper were attracted toward the comb.

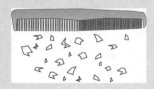

1. What force attracted the scraps of paper toward the comb?

   A. Magnetic   **B.** Frictional

   C. Centripetal   **D.** Electrostatic

Crop-dusting planes release pesticide through electrostatic spray nozzles in order to minimize pesticide waste. The centre of each spray nozzle contains a needle with a positive charge. Droplets of the pesticide become charged when the make contact with the needle on their way past the needle and out of the nozzle. When the charged droplets fall onto the leaves of the crop, the droplets are less likely to be carried away by the wind.

2. The charged droplets are not likely to blow off of the leaves because the charged droplets

    A. gain electrons from the air and transfer them to the leaves

    B. fall faster through the air because they have similar charges

    C. repel each other and spread out, minimizing the effect of the wind

    D. induce an opposite charge on the leaves to form an attraction between them

Open Response

3. Kara wanted to demonstrate electrostatic electricity to her class. First, she turned on the water tap slightly in order to obtain a slow moving stream of water. Then, she blew up a balloon and rubbed it on her dry hair several times. Finally, Kara held the balloon near the running water without touching the balloon to the water. The stream of water bent toward the balloon. Using the law of electrical charges, explain the reason that the stream of water bent toward the balloon.

_____

_____

_____

_____

_____

9.4.1.2 *compare qualitatively static and current electricity*

COMPARING STATIC AND CURRENT ELECTRICITY

Static electricity is the build up, or accumulation, of electric charges in an object. Current electricity is the flow, or movement, of electric charges within a circuit.

STATIC ELECTRICITY

Static electricity is the build up or loss of electrons by the transfer of electrons from one object to another. When a charge stays in place for some length of time it is described as static electricity.

An electroscope is a device used to detect the presence of static electricity. The electroscope is usually constructed with a metal plate or sphere at the top of a metal post, with two thin foil leaves hanging from the bottom of the post. This setup is typically supported in a flask or some other transparent enclosure. If a charged object is brought near the top of the electroscope, the foil leaves repel one another and they spread apart. The greater the charge from the object, the farther apart the leaves move.

Charges are not energy, they are electrons and protons, part of the matter that make up all atoms.

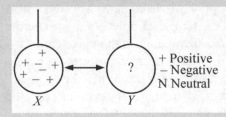

CURRENT ELECTRICITY

Current electricity is the flow of charges within a circuit. The charges flow from an area of high energy to an area of low energy.

Current electricity refers to the controlled flow of electric charges through a conductor. An electric circuit is a continuous, looping path, formed by a conductor, for electricity to flow through. Electricity flows along a conductor from an energy source, such as a battery, to a device that uses the energy, such as a light bulb.

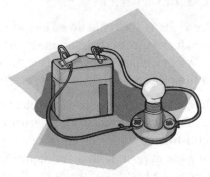

Practice

Use the following information to answer the next question.

As Joshua closed his car door, he received a small shock. The shock was caused by a buildup of __*i*__ electricity; the resulting spark is called a __*ii*__.

4. The information in which of the following tables completes the given statement?

A.

i	*ii*
current	discharge

B.

i	*ii*
static	charge

C.

i	*ii*
current	charge

D.

i	*ii*
static	discharge

Use the following information to answer the next question.

When balloons X and Y were suspended from the ceiling in a science classroom, they moved away from each other.

+ Positive
− Negative
N Neutral

5. Which of the following diagrams represents the charge on balloon Y in order for the two balloons to repel each other?

A.

B.

C.

D.

Open Response

6. What is the difference between static and current electricity?

_____

_____

_____

_____

_____

_____

_____

_____

9.4.1.3 *describe the concepts of electric current, potential difference, and resistance, with the help of a water analogy*

ELECTRIC CURRENT, POTENTIAL DIFFERENCE, AND RESISTANCE

It is impossible to directly observe many of the properties of electricity, such as electric current, potential difference, and resistance. Usually, these properties are only observed by careful measurement of the effects caused by the properties. Therefore, to help understand these properties, scientists use the "water analogy" to explain these concepts.

POTENTIAL DIFFERENCE (VOLTAGE)

Voltage is the potential difference (current drop) between two points in a circuit. It is the push, or pressure, behind the current flow. Voltage is measured with a voltmeter in volt units.

To describe the potential difference using the water analogy, consider the difference in the potential energy of water dropping over a waterfall. The higher the waterfall, the larger the potential difference of the water. This causes the water to flow faster at the bottom of the waterfall.

CURRENT

Current refers to the quantity of electrons flowing in a circuit and the rate at which these electrons flow. A strong current is measured with an ammeter in ampere units. A weak current is measured with a galvanometer in milliampere units.

To describe the current using the water analogy, consider that a fast moving river has more water flow per second past a given point than a slow moving river.

RESISTANCE

Resistance is the measure of the difficulty electrons have flowing through a substance. The higher the resistance, the more work must be done by the electrons to travel through the substance. This converts some of the electrical energy into other forms of energy, such as light and heat energy.

For example, the electrons must work much harder to move through a tungsten filament in a light bulb than they do to move along a copper wire. As a result, some of the electrical energy converts into light energy and heat energy. Commercial resistors are used to control current and voltage flow. A high resistance allows only a small current to flow through a component. A low resistance allows a large current to flow through. Resistance is measured in ohm units.

To describe the current using the water analogy, consider the flow of water in a river as it passes through a rocky channel. The rocks create resistance to the flowing water, so less water passes through the rocky section, and the water will flow slower on the other side of the rocks.

CHALLENGER QUESTION
Use the following information to answer the next question.

Water in a tank is used to keep a vegetable garden moist. The pressure in the tank is low but it can be increased by adding more water to the tank.

7. This situation is an analogy for which of the following electrical concepts?

A. Power   B. Current

C. Voltage   D. Resistance

Use the following information to answer the next question.

In a water distribution system, water flows through tubes and pipes as a result of the difference in the pressure at different positions, called the pressure gradient.

8. If the given water distribution system were used as analogy for an electric circuit, then what would be the electric charge?

   A. Pressure difference

   B. Water flow

   C. Water

   D. Pipes

Open Response

Use the following information to answer the next question.

A mountain river leads over a 10 m tall cliff, creating a waterfall. After the waterfall, the river continues to flow rapidly along a narrow river bed. Eventually, the river bed widens and the water slows down. Then the water has to pass by an obstacle of large boulders.

9. Use the given water analogy to describe voltage, current, and resistance in an electrical system.

9.4.1.4 *explain how electric current, potential difference, and resistance are measured using an ammeter and a voltmeter*

MEASURING ELECTRIC CURRENT, POTENTIAL DIFFERENCE, AND RESISTANCE

Meters are measuring instruments. An ammeter measures current, a voltmeter measures the potential difference between two points, and an ohmmeter measures resistance. All of these devices are metres, and they are very similar in design. However, metres can be analog (needle pointing to a dial) or digital (a numerical value displayed directly).

A voltmeter

When connecting a metre to an electric circuit, remember the following rules:

1. Connect positive to positive and negative to negative

2. Negative terminals = Black

3. Positive terminals = Red

AMMETER

An ammeter measures the amount of electric current flowing in a circuit. To measure the electric current, the ammeter is connected directly into the circuit in which the measured current flows. To do this, disconnect a wire in the circuit and connect the ammeter in series with the circuit. An ammeter has a very low resistance. Electric currents are measured in amperes (A) or milliamperes (mA).

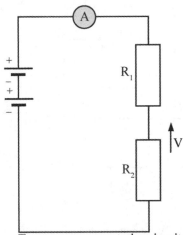

To measure current, the circuit must be broken to allow the ammeter to be connected in series

VOLTMETER

A voltmeter is used to measure voltages. A voltmeter can be connected in parallel across the terminals of a cell to measure the voltage output of the cell, or in parallel across another component of a circuit to measure the voltage drop across this component. A voltmeter should have a very high resistance.

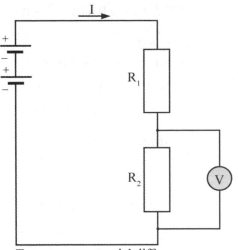

To measure potential difference, the voltmeter is connected in parallel.

OHMMETERS

An ohmmeter tests resistance by passing a small current through a circuit component and measuring the voltage produced. To measure resistance, the component must be removed from the circuit altogether.

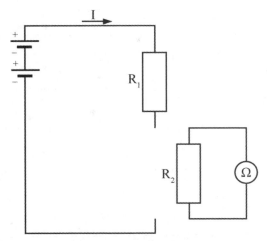

To measure resistance, the component is removed from the circuit.

SUMMARY OF ELECTRICAL TERMS

Electrical Term	Definition
Current	Rate of flow
Voltage	Force of flow
Resistance	Opposition to flow

Unit of Measurement	Symbol
Ampere	A
Volt	V
Ohm	Ω

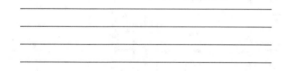

 Practice

Open Response

10. What does an ammeter measure? How would you connect an ammeter to a component of a circuit that you wish to measure?

_____

_____

_____

_____

_____

CHALLENGER QUESTION

11. Which of the following circuit diagrams shows the correct placement of a voltmeter for measuring the electric potential energy across lamp B?

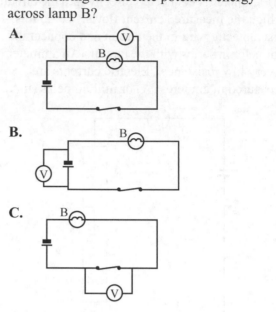

9.4.1.5 *describe qualitatively the effects of varying electrical resistance and potential difference on electric current in an electrical circuit;*

9.4.1.6 *apply the relationship potential difference = resistance × current resistance current to simple series circuits*

POTENTIAL DIFFERENCE AND ELECTRICAL RESISTANCE

Potential difference, also called the voltage, is a measurement of pressure. This pressure is the drop in potential between two ends of the conductor through which the current flows. The potential drop is the difference in energy between the positive pole and the negative pole in a cell. The unit for measuring potential difference is the volt (V), using a voltmeter.

Resistance is a property that restricts the flow of electrons through a substance. Resistance is affected by the voltage. A higher voltage means a higher resistance. Resistance is measured in ohms (Ω) using an ohmmeter.

OHM'S LAW

German scientist Georg Ohm developed a law that linked voltage, current, and resistance together. This law, now called Ohm's law, states that the current flowing through a wire varies directly with the voltage applied to the wire. This means the more voltage leads to more current.

Ohm's Law also relates resistance to current. If the resistance increases in a circuit, the current decreases. This means the resistance varies indirectly with the current.

Therefore, Ohm's law can be written as:

Volts(V) = Current(I) × Resistance(R)
$$V = I \times R$$

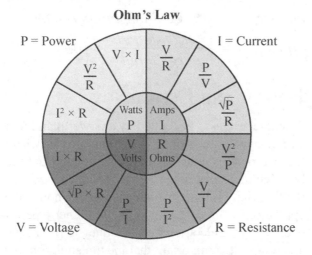

Ohm's Law

P = Power   I = Current

V = Voltage   R = Resistance

To help remember the formula, cover the letter in the above diagram you are trying to solve for and that will reveal the formula you should use!

Knowing any two of the values makes it possible to calculate the third. Current can be determined by using the formula:

$$I = \frac{V}{R}$$

Resistance can be determined by using the formula:

$$R = \frac{V}{I}$$

1. What is the voltage of the power source that has a 1.5 A current flowing through a 30 Ω lamp resistance?
   Solution:

   $V = I \times R$
   $V = 1.5 \text{ A} \times 30 \text{ }\Omega$
   $V = 45 \text{ V}$

   The power source has a voltage of 45 V.

2. A hair dryer produces a resistance of 12 Ω when plugged into a 110 V electrical outlet. How much current passes through the dryer?
   Solution:

   $$I = \frac{V}{R}$$
   $$I = \frac{110 \text{ V}}{12 \text{ }\Omega}$$
   $I = 9.2 \text{ A}$

   The hair dryer has a current of 9.2 A.

3. A radio uses a current of 0.2 A when operated by a 9 V battery. What is the resistance in the radio circuit?
   Solution:

   $$R = \frac{V}{I}$$
   $$R = \frac{9 \text{ V}}{0.2 \text{ A}}$$
   $R = 45 \text{ }\Omega$

   The resistance in the circuit is 45 Ω.

Practice

Use the following information to answer the next question.

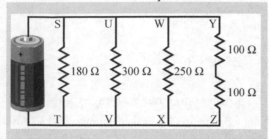

12. The electrical pathway that has the highest current is between points

 A. S and T   **B.** U and V

 C. W and X   **D.** Y and Z

13. Jason can calculate voltage (V) in an electrical circuit when he is given the resistance (R) and current (I) for a light bulb connected to the circuit. If both the resistance of the light and the current passing through the light are doubled, then the new voltage will represented by

 A. $V \times 2$ **B.** $V \times 4$

 C. $\dfrac{V}{2}$ **D.** $\dfrac{V}{4}$

Use the following information to answer the next question.

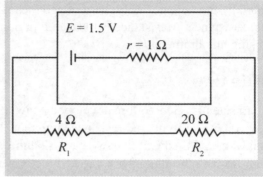

14. A 1.5 V cell with an internal resistance of $1\ \Omega$ is connected in series to resistors of $4\ \Omega$ and $20\ \Omega$. What is the current in the circuit?

 A. 0.05 A   **B.** 0.06 A

 C. 0.08 A   **D.** 0.12 A

9.4.1.7 *determine quantitatively the percent efficiency of an electrical device that converts electrical energy to other forms of energy, using the relationship percent*

$$efficiency = \frac{energy\ output}{energy\ input} \times 100$$

POWER AND EFFICIENCY

After electricity is generated by a power plant, it is carried by transmission lines to transformers, where the electricity is reduced to a usable voltage that can be safely used in a home to run appliances. When the electricity is used by appliances in the home, the appliances change the electricity into other types of energy. Since electricity costs money to produce and to use, it is important that the transmission of electricity to the home and the usage of electricity in the home is efficient.

POWER

Power is the rate at which a device converts energy. It is measured in watts (W). Electric power is dependent on voltage and current.

Power = Voltage × Current
(watts) (volts)   (amps)

Power is also defined as the energy per unit time. Power describes the amount of one form of energy that is converted into other forms, such as light, heat, and sound.

Power = energy / time

Formula: $P = \dfrac{E}{t}$

$1 \text{ Watt} = \dfrac{1 \text{ Joule}}{1 \text{ second}}$

watts = joules / second

where Joule is the unit for measuring energy (J).

EFFICIENCY

Efficiency refers to the amount of productive work, or the amount of work done that is used for its correct purpose. This means that when electrical energy is converted into other types of energy, the amount of energy that is not lost is used efficiently. However, when a device changes energy into heat, the efficiency decreases. Efficiency is expressed as a percentage, and is determined by dividing the output energy by the input energy.

Many appliances used today are more energy efficient than those of the past. A fridge today uses much less power and is much more efficient.

Efficiency is measured as the ratio of the useful energy output to the total energy input. For example, the efficiency of an incandescent light bulb is much less than that of an equivalent fluorescent light bulb because an incandescent bulb produces a lot of heat. The useful energy output of an incandescent bulb is much less compared to the total input energy.

Formula: $\text{Efficiency} = \dfrac{\text{Output Energy}}{\text{Input Energy}} \times 100$

Example

An incandescent light bulb uses 780 J of energy to produce 21 J of light. What is the efficiency of the light bulb?

Solution:

$\text{Efficiency} = \dfrac{\text{Output Energy}}{\text{Input Energy}} \times 100$

$\text{Efficiency} = \dfrac{31 \text{ J}}{780 \text{ J}} \times 100$

$\text{Efficiency} = 4\%$

An incandescent light bulb is 4% efficient in producing light. The remaining 96% is converted into heat, which is lost energy. A fluorescent light bulb is about 22% efficient. Approximately 78% of its energy is lost as heat.

An incandescent light bulb and a fluorescent light bulb

Electric motors are more efficient that gas-fuelled combustion engines. Electric motors have fewer moving parts that waste energy as heat. There has been a gradual increase in the number of motorist using electric vehicles across Canada.

All appliances sold in Canada must carry an "EnerGuide" label that indicates the electrical consumption of the appliance. Usually, a number on the label in kilowatt-hours indicates the average power per year consumption of the appliance.

Practice

15. When calculating the efficiency of a home appliance, the ratio of the input energy to the output energy is multiplied by

A. 1   B. 10

C. 100   D. 1 000

Use the following information to answer the next question.

Andrew buys an electric generator. The generator uses 12 000 J of fuel energy to generate 6 800 J of electrical energy.

16. What is the efficiency of the generator?

A. 50.3%   B. 54.6%

C. 56.7%   D. 58.5%

9.4.2.1a *"through investigations and applications of basic concepts:— demonstrate knowledge of electrical safety procedures when planning and carrying out investigations and choosing and using materials, tools, and equipment"*

ELECTRICAL SAFETY PROCEDURES

Electricity can kill a person, so it must be treated with respect at all times. As a student, the electricity that you will be exposed to in the classroom is always within safe limits. However, as soon as you leave your classroom, situations will exist that can expose you to harmful and even fatal amounts of electricity. Learn about and use safe practices when working with electricity, so that you can react properly when faced with a potentially dangerous situation.

GENERAL RULES FOR WORKING WITH ELECTRICITY

1. Know the voltages and amperages of the electricity that you work with.

2. Handle live wires only if you know the source of electricity is safe.

3. Do not plug any electrical device into a wall outlet if the cords are damaged in any way, if the copper wires are exposed, or the third prong (the ground) has been broken or removed from the plug.

4. Avoid mixing water and electricity under any circumstances.

5. If you are working with electricity coming from a wall outlet, be aware that this amount of electricity can kill you. Avoid standing in water, touching metal plumbing pipes, metal counter tops, or any other conductors that could cause the electricity to pass through your body on its way to ground.

The majority of electrocutions occur in industrial accidents, using faulty power tools or making contact with high voltage sources (such as overhead power lines). Be careful!

High voltage overhead power lines

ELECTRICAL DANGER

There is a great deal of confusion about the dangers of electricity. Electrical current is often expressed as a voltage or an amperage. If either number is high the electric current can be dangerous.

One rule of thumb is "it is the volts that jolt, but it is the amps that kill." This is not a bad rule of thumb because high current (large amperage) will always be dangerous. However, it is impossible to simplify the situation like this, because the voltage of the electricity can also be a factor. A person could die from only 1 A if the voltage is high enough.

Resistance to electricity is also a factor. Dry skin can offer as much as 100 000 ohms of resistance. However, if the skin is wet or there is an open wound, then the resistance of the skin can drop to as little as 1 000 ohms. If electricity can pass through the skin, the rest of the body forms a good conductor. Electricity passing through body organs is the major cause of death by electrocution.

Lightning strikes

Electricity can also travel along someone's skin without ever penetrating the body. This can still cause severe damage in the form of burns to the skin.

Another factor is the duration of electrical shock, or how long the body is exposed to the electricity. Continuous exposure to electrical current is more dangerous than a very brief shock or discharge of electricity. This is only a general rule, however. Even a brief shock can cause the heart to stop beating, which will lead to death if the heart does not restart. As well, someone standing on a ladder could fall because of an electrical shock and be hurt as a consequence.

High voltage sources can be dangerous for entirely different reasons. Electricity can jump across space if it has enough voltage, reaching a body that is near the electricity source. It is not necessary to touch the source because the high voltage electricity will leap to anything that offers it an easy path to reach the ground. For that reason, high voltage sources always have fences around them to keep people away.

High voltage can jump across space

Your best defense against being hurt by electricity is to treat electricity with the respect it deserves. Use electrical devices properly and safely and they will serve you well.

Practice

17. What are two devices that are commonly used in electric appliances to provide electrical safety?

   A. A transformer and an ammeter

   B. A generator and a voltmeter

   C. A fuse and a ground wire

   D. A voltmeter and a battery

9.4.2.1b - *identify an authentic practical challenge or problem related to the use of electricity*

PROBLEMS RELATED TO ELECTRICITY USAGE

As electricity becomes a larger necessity in society, more issues regarding its usage are developing. There are concerns with when energy is used, how much is used, and methods for delivering it as resources become more scarce.

PEAK ENERGY USE

Electrical distribution systems are designed to deliver electricity to all customers connected to the system. The capacity of the system to make electricity should be able to supply the electrical needs of everyone. However, there are periods of time when too many users want to consume large amounts of electricity at the same time. These time periods are referred to as peak usage periods. If the electricity generation cannot keep up with the demand, electrical brown outs or complete system failures may result. This means that parts of the system, or possibly everyone connected to the system, will be cut off from electricity.

Brainstorm some reasons why electrical demand would peak at certain hours of the day or certain times of the year.

PERSONAL ENERGY USE

Consider how much electricity your family uses at home. If everyone could reduce their energy consumption, major benefits would occur as a result. These benefits would include:

- Cost savings—your parents would have to pay less on their power bills
- Lower demand—power companies would not have to produce as much electricity, and they could delay building new, very expensive power generating plants until later
- Less pollution—much electricity is generated by burning coal or natural gas; less electricity demand means less coal or gas is burned to generate electricity and fewer greenhouse gases are emitted.

Everyone could reduce energy consumption in their homes by replacing regular incandescent bulbs with compact fluorescent bulbs. Research the benefits and savings that compact fluorescent bulbs can provide.

Research how much energy consumption certain appliances have. Compare these figures with the energy consumption of new, more energy efficient models. Calculate how much energy could be saved every year if certain appliances were replaced with newer, more energy efficient models.

ALUMINIUM VS. COPPER WIRE

Recently, aluminium wiring was used in newly constructed homes. Problems with the aluminium wires began to surface, and aluminium wiring fell out of favour.

Research the use of aluminium for electrical wiring. What was the reason for using aluminium instead of copper for wires? What problems did aluminium wiring cause?

:Practice

18. Considering the basic principles of electric circuits, household electrical appliances should be connected

   A. in series

   B. in parallel

   C. in series and in parallel

   D. neither in series nor in parallel

9.4.2.1c - *formulate questions about the problem or issue*

SCIENTIFIC QUESTIONS ABOUT ELECTRICITY

To help you understand why efficiency is so important, you could determine how much energy is consumed in your home, and then determine how much that energy costs. You can accomplish this by performing certain tests to determine energy consumption, and then multiplying these values with current energy prices. You can determine how much your family's total electricity consumption is over a period of time, or you could establish how much electricity is used by a particular appliance or set of appliances.

DETERMINING ELECTRICAL ENERGY CONSUMPTION

Record electricity metre readings for a set period of time, either two or four weeks. Calculate the cost of the energy used by multiplying the consumption by the current rate at which electricity is being charged.

Determine the energy consumption of a household appliance by determining the amount of energy used by the device (see the panel on the device or motor to find data for the energy usage of the appliance).

How much energy could be saved by

1. changing your energy consumption habits?

2. replacing certain appliances with newer energy efficient ones?

9.4.2.1d - *demonstrate the skills required to plan and conduct an inquiry into the use of electricity, using instruments, tools, and apparatus safely, accurately, and effectively*

STUDYING ELECTRICITY USAGE

How much energy is used by home appliances?

Develop a list of appliances for comparing. Check the nameplate on the bottom or at the back of each appliance. On certain appliances, it may be necessary to look at the manufacturer's label on the motor to get information. The maximum amount of power the appliance draws is the wattage of the appliance. This value is a number needed to calculate how much electricity the appliance uses.

CALCULATE THE ANNUAL COST

The following formula can be used to calculate the amount of energy an appliance uses in one year.

$$\frac{\text{watts} \times \text{daily use} \times \text{days}}{1\ 000} = \text{kWh}$$

The result is in units called kilowatt-hours (kWh). One kilowatt-hour is the amount of electricity it would take to operate a 1 000 W electrical device for one hour. Ten devices operating at 10 W for one hour would also consume 1 kWh. A 100 W light bulb will use 100 W of energy in one hour. If that bulb burns for 10 hours, then it will use 1 000 watts, or 1 kWh.

:Example

If Cheng uses an electric heater (800 watts) for two hours each day for 60 days per year, what will it cost him to run the heater for the year if his electricity cost is 12.9 cents per kWh?

Solution:

$$\frac{800\ \text{W} \times 2\ \text{h} \times 60\ \text{d}}{1\ 000} = 96\ \text{kWh}$$

96 kWh × 12.9 cents / kWh = 1 238 cents per year

Cheng's annual cost to operate the heater is $12.38.

APPLIANCES AND WATTAGE

The following table provides sample data for doing energy consumption calculations.

Appliance	Wattage
Refrigerator	1 580–1 800
Coffee maker	800–1 100
Alarm clock	10
Microwave	600–1 200
Washing machine	300–500
Clothes dryer	1 800–4 000

Practice

Open Response

*Use the following information to
answer the next question.*

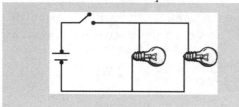

19. Indicate on the given diagram where you
    would connect a voltmeter if you wanted
    to measure the voltage flowing through the
    outer light bulb.

    _____

    _____

9.4.2.1e - *select and integrate information
from various sources, including electronic
and print resources, community resources,
and personally collected data, to answer the
questions chosen*

PERSONALLY COLLECTED DATA

By building circuits and then testing them for
voltage, current, and resistance can teach you a great
deal about how circuits work. These types of
investigations fall under the category of personally
collected data. The hands-on experience is a
powerful tool for learning, and the results from
doing it yourself can stick with you better that just
textbook learning alone.

In order to create a personal electricity lab, collect
together the following components:

- electrical wires
- 1.5 V batteries
- 1.5 V bulbs in socket holders
- 1.5 V toy motors
- resistors
- electrical tape
- an inexpensive multimeter

If at all possible, obtain some wire leads that have
alligator clips attached to each end. These are very
useful for making quick connections and leave only
a small amount of bare metal exposed, allowing the
multimeter probes to touch the circuit in order to
take readings.

Devise circuits and circuit testing procedures to
study the following electrical principles:

1. Battery tester: use the voltmeter function on the
   multimeter to determine how powerful each of
   your batteries is. Label the batteries with their
   actual voltage for future reference. If you use the
   batteries a lot, test them frequently.

2. Batteries in series vs. parallel circuits: set up
   simple circuits that will power a load, either a
   bulb or motor. Arrange two or more batteries into
   parallel and series circuits, and take voltage and
   amperage readings of the circuits to see what
   effect the arrangement of batteries has.

3. Light bulbs in parallel and series circuits: repeat the process above, except use only one battery and two or more lightbulbs. Take readings of voltage and amperage at different points in the circuit. Try unscrewing one light bulb to see what effect this "short circuit" has on the other bulbs.

4. Resistance: place a resistor into a circuit containing a motor or lightbulb load. Place the resistor before the load, after the load, and across the two wires that lead into and out of the load. Determine what effect the resistor has on the electrical current that goes through the load.

The given circuit diagrams show two circuits, one with the batteries connected in series and the other in parallel. Before testing the circuit, ask yourself which type of battery arrangement will generate the highest voltage in the circuit and which arrangement will produce the highest current? By testing the circuits with the multimeter the answers to these questions can be found.

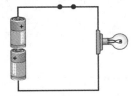 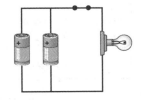

Batteries in series   *Batteries in parallel*

9.4.2.1f - *organize, record, and analyse the information gathered*

PROCESSING DATA

When conducting investigations, it is important to record the data collected and then analyzing the data. Without this, an investigator only have multiple procedures, readings, and results. It would be difficult to conclude anything about electricity from the investigation. For that reason, it is important to create an orderly procedure, to follow the procedure in order, and then to analyze the results.

Apply the following principles to the circuit building and testing process:

1. Determine which question is being asked in each test. Form a hypothesis about what will happen before any readings are taken.

2. Record your results for each test. Draw a circuit diagram and label the positions of the multimeter probes for each test on the diagram. Number or letter each probe location and indicate the position in a data table. A sample data table is provided below.

SAMPLE DATA TABLE

Probe Location	Voltage (V)	Amperage (A)
A–A		
B–B		

3. Perform each test and record results in the appropriate spaces, or make notes about the results if there is something that you want to remember for later use. (For example, adding a third light bulb in parallel caused all of the bulbs to dim slightly)

4. Look at the results and attempt to use the readings to answer the question. The hypothesis might be right or wrong. That does not matter. It is the idea behind what happened to the electrical current in each part of the circuit that is important.

5. Write down a conclusion that summarizes the answer to the question.

9.4.2.1g - *communicate scientific ideas, procedures, results, and conclusions using appropriate SI units, language, and formats*

COMMUNICATING SCIENTIFIC IDEAS

The study of electricity has a language all it's own. The words that we use to describe electricity are an attempt to describe amounts, to put numbers and mathematics to work to show what is happening.

The fundamental units of electricity and the related SI unit and symbol is given below.

	SI Unit	Symbol
Current	Ampere (amp)	A
Voltage	Volt	V
Wattage	Watt	W
Resistance	Ohm	Ω

These units have mathematical relationships that allow calculations to be made to determine unknown values.

$$\text{Voltage} = \text{Resistance} \times \text{Current}$$

$$\text{Resistance} = \frac{\text{Voltage}}{\text{Current}}$$

$$\text{Current} = \frac{\text{Voltage}}{\text{Resistance}}$$

$$\text{Wattage} = \text{Current} \times \text{Voltage}$$

$$\text{Current} = \frac{\text{Wattage}}{\text{Voltage}}$$

$$\text{Voltage} = \frac{\text{Wattage}}{\text{Current}}$$

9.4.2.2 *design, draw, and construct series and parallel circuits that perform a specific function*

SERIES AND PARALLEL CIRCUITS

An electrical circuit is a system composed of four components or subsystems.

Component	Example
Power Source	110 V outlet, battery, cell
Conductor	Copper wire
Load	Light, motor, resistor
Control	Switch

In order to better understand how a circuit is made, a schematic diagram is often drawn. A schematic diagram serves as a blueprint of the circuit.

Standard electrical symbols are used to construct schematic diagrams. Here are the basic electrical components and their symbols

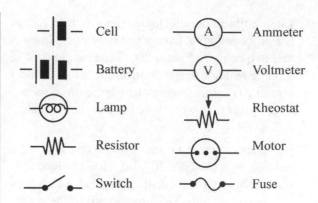

SERIES CIRCUITS

A series circuit has one current pathway. Electrons leave the negative (−) pole of the cell, passes through all the subsystems in the single path, and enter back into the cell through the positive (+) pole.

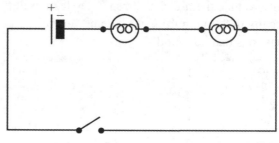

Series circuit

In the past, Christmas lights were wired in series. If one light burned out, none of the other lights would work. This is because the electricity cannot flow past the burned out bulb. In the series circuit above, the energy from the power source is used by the two lights at the same time. The lights must share the energy. As a result each bulb lights less brightly than if only one bulb were connected to the power source.

PARALLEL CIRCUIT

A parallel circuit has more than one current pathway. Electrons still leave negative (−) pole and return to the positive (+) pole of the cell, but the electrons take different paths as they travel through the components.

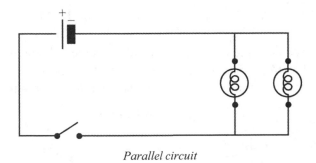

Parallel circuit

Your house is wired as a parallel circuit. If one light burns out, the others remain lit. Each light in a parallel circuit shines with the same brightness because each bulb has a different electrical path that provides the same amount of energy.

Practice

Use the following information to answer the next question.

Owen constructs two electrical circuits. Each circuit consists of two bulbs, two switches, and a battery. The two circuits constructed by Owen are indicated by Figures I and II.

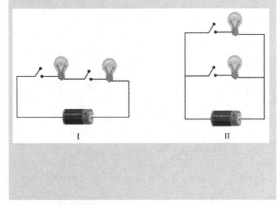

20. Which of the following statements explains what will happen if one switch is closed in each of the circuits?

A. Both bulbs will glow in circuit I and only one bulb will glow in circuit II.

B. Neither bulb will glow in circuit I and only one bulb will glow in circuit II.

C. Only one bulb will glow in circuit I and neither bulb will glow in circuit II.

D. Only one bulb will glow in circuit I and only one bulb will glow in circuit II.

9.4.2.3 *use appropriate instruments to collect and graph data, and determine the relationship between voltage and current in a simple series circuit with a single resistor*

VOLTAGE AND CURRENT

Consider a circuit made up of a resistor, an electric cell, a switch, an ammeter, and a voltmeter. A schematic diagram of the circuit would look like this:

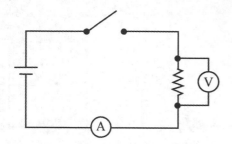

Voltage versus current schematic

If this circuit was used in an experiment, it would be possible to find the voltage of the electric cell and see the relationship between the voltage and current in a simple series circuit with a single resistor. Even without setting this experiment up, it is possible to come to a conclusion using Ohm's law.

$$V = I \times R$$

Suppose the resistor in the above schematic diagram has a value of 54 Ω and is connected to a 1.5 V electric cell. Once the switch is closed, the voltmeter would measure the voltage across the resistor as 1.5 V. Ohm's law can then be used to calculate the current.

$$\left(I = \frac{V}{R}\right)$$

An ammeter could also be used to find the value of the current. The current in this circuit should be 0.028 amperes. If more electric cells were added in series to the circuit, the voltage would increase for each added cell. The new current could be measured or calculated. The following table displays the results of adding extra electric cells to the described circuit:

# of Electric Cells in the Circuit	Voltage (V)	Current (A)
1	1.5	0.028
2	3.0	0.056
3	4.5	0.083
4	6.0	0.111

According to the data in this table, as the voltage in the circuit increases, so does the current. A more visual method to display this data is to use a graph.

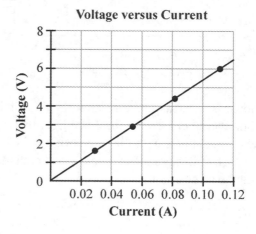

Since the relationship is linear, a best-fit line (straight line) can be drawn through the data.

Since the current increases as the voltage increases, there is a direct relationship between the current and the voltage. This means that the voltage is directly related to the current.

9.4.2.4 *charge an electroscope by contact and by induction*

THE ELECTROSCOPE

An electroscope is a device used to detect the presence of electrostatic charge and it's relative amount. There are two methods for charging an electroscope: by contact or induction.

CONTACT

One method of charging an electroscope is by contact, or conduction. This means that a charged object actually touches the electroscope, and charge transfers from the object to the electroscope. If the electroscope returns to normal after being touched by the charged object, then it is likely that the charged object is so weakly charged that it is not willing to share its excess charge with the electroscope.

When charging the electroscope by contact, it is important to note the following properties:
– the charged object and electroscope become charged alike
– the charged object must actually touch the electroscope and transfer some electrons to it
– the charged object becomes less charged because it actually lost some charge; therefore, there is a limit to how many times it can be used to charge other objects without being recharged

INDUCTION

The other method for charging an electroscope is to bring a charged object near the electroscope without touching the electroscope. The presence of the charged object above the plate of the electroscope induces the electrons within the electroscope to move accordingly. Then, with the charged object still held above the plate, the electroscope is touched. At this point the electrons will flow between the electroscope and the ground, giving the electroscope a charge. Grounding the electroscope will cause the leaves to close. When the charged object is moved away, the leaves will spread again, but now the electroscope is charged with a polarity that is opposite to the charge in the object.

Induction, before electroscope is touched.

When charging the electroscope by induction, it is important to note the following properties:
– the charged object does not touch the electroscope
– the first charge is strong and stays strong each time the electroscope is recharged
– the electroscope ends up with a charge oppositive to the charge of the object used to charge it

9.4.3.1 *describe and explain household wiring and its typical components*

9.4.3.2 *develop a solution to a practical problem related to the use of electricity in the home, school, or community*

HOUSEHOLD WIRING

There are two or more paths for the electrons to travel in a parallel circuit. However, the voltage is the same in each branch. If a switch were opened in one branch of the circuit, the current would continue flowing through the other branches.

The current within a circuit is equal to the sum of the currents required by each of the appliances in the circuit. As the number of appliances connected to the circuit increases, the total current in the circuit also increases. If the current becomes too large, the circuit cannot meet the demand. This means that the circuit is overloaded, and the wires can overheat and start a fire.

To prevent a circuit from overloading, fuses or circuit breakers are built into most circuits. A fuse is made with a metal wire that has a low melting point. When the current is greater than the rating of the fuse, the wire melts and the current is stopped. The flow of electricity will not begin again until a new fuse is put into the circuit. However, the cause of the overload must be found and corrected first.

Fuse

New homes use circuit breakers instead of fuses. A circuit breaker looks like a light switch. When too much current flows through a breaker, the circuit is opened. When the circuit has cooled, the breaker can be resent. However, a breaker should never be reset without locating the cause of the overload and correcting it.

:Example

One morning when Sasha tried to blow dry her hair in her bedroom, her father used his electric razor in the bathroom right next door at the same time. Both the blow dryer and the razor stopped working. Did both appliances break down at the exact same time?

Solution:

No, the appliances did not break down. The appliances quit working because too much current overloaded the circuit. The breaker would have to be resent or the fuse replaced and both Sasha and her father would have to remember not to use their appliances at the same time in the future.

Both fuses and circuit breakers protect a building from short circuits. A short circuit occurs when the current takes a short cut and does not follow its intended path. If a short circuit occurred, there would be a large increase in the circuit's current. The wire in the fuse would then melt, or the circuit breaker would activate and the circuit would be broken.

:Practice

21. A fuse is a safety device that protects an electrical circuit from overheating. A fuse is located in a fuse box and is connected to the circuit in

   A. series

   B. parallel

   C. a combination of parallel followed by series

   D. a combination of series followed by parallel

Use the following information to answer the next question.

As a safety feature, a device should be inserted into the given circuit to prevent a power surge that would burn the lights out.

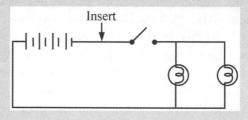

22. Which of the following devices should be inserted into the existing circuit?

   A. -\/\/\/-   **B.** -(•••)-

   C. ⌒⌒   **D.** -(V)-

9.4.3.3 *compare electrical energy production technologies, including risks and benefits*

RENEWABLE ENERGY SOURCES

Electricity can be generated by many different means. Traditionally, electricity is generated by non-renewable resources, such as gas and coal. However, as non-renewable resources become depleted, alternate energy sources for generating electricity must be considered. There are many alternatives to the traditional fossil fuel generated power.

HYDRO POWER

Hydroelectricity, or water power, is generated in areas where large volumes of water are collected behind dams. The collected water stores a high potential energy. When the water passes through a channel in the dam, the moving water spins turbines in the dam, which turns a generator to produce electricity.

Hydroelectric power plant

SOLAR ENERGY

Solar energy is energy given off by the sun. The amount of solar energy that reaches Earth in a 40-minute time period is equal to the amount of energy used by humans on Earth in one year! The potential for the use of this type of energy is immense. Solar energy is a renewable source of energy. At the present time, this energy can be used in a number of ways, as shown in the diagrams.

Solar panels convert solar energy into stored electrical energy.

Solar powered satellites collect solar energy.

Solar energy used directly to heat homes or cook food.

WIND POWER

Windmills or wind turbines generate electricity in high-wind areas. Although the initial cost of construction is high, wind energy is a renewable resource. One windmill is capable of generating enough power to meet the needs of approximately 20 homes.

TIDAL GENERATORS

Tidal generators use water currents to produce electricity. Huge tidal waves spin specially designed turbine generators to produce electricity. Waves are a good source of energy because they are readily available. However, the force of the waves are inconsistent because they are affected by the changing gravitational pull of the moon. Tidal power is a relatively new concept and is in the experimental stages of development. Tidal power is used generated in the Bay of Fundy, providing a portion of Nova Scotia's required electricity.

Practice

23. The **main** advantage of using nuclear energy to produce electrical power is that it
    A. provides more energy per unit of fuel consumed
    B. produces the highest-quality of electricity
    C. uses a readily available uranium fuel
    D. releases radiation as a by-product

24. The International Space Station is a structure constructed 300 km above Earth's surface to provide living accommodation for scientists studying conditions in space. What is the **main** source of electrical energy used to power the space station?
    A. Wind energy
    B. Solar energy
    C. Water energy
       Nuclear energy

9.4.3.4 *explain how some common household electrical appliances operate*

ELECTRICAL APPLIANCES

Everyday, households rely on electricity to operate. Meals are made in microwaves and ovens, laundry is done in the washing machine and dryer, and dishes are washed in the dishwasher. Electricity allows for many conveniences that did not exist one century ago.

Household electrical appliances operate on a circuit. The four parts of a circuit are:

1. power supply
2. conductor
3. control
4. load

An electric frying pan plugs into an electrical outlet (power supply). The current travels through one of the wires (conductor) in the cord to a switch (control) on the handle, through the heating element (load) in the pan, out through the second wire in the cord (conductor), and back to the outlet (power supply). This is a complete circuit. All household electrical appliances operate in this manner.

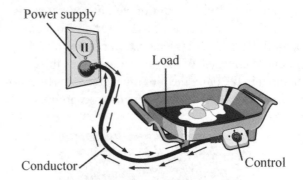

Practice

25. Which of the following energy conversions takes place in an electric heater?
    A. Heat energy → sound energy
    B. Heat energy → electric energy
    C. Electric energy → heat energy
    D. Mechanical energy → electric energy

26. Which of the following characteristics should devices such as electric light bulbs, electric kettles, and electric heaters have?
    A. High resistance   B. Low resistance
    C. Low power   D. Large size

9.4.3.5 *describe careers that involve electrical technologies, and use employability assessment programs, newspaper job advertisements, and/or appropriate Internet sources to identify the knowledge and skill requirements of such careers*

CAREERS IN ELECTRICAL TECHNOLOGY

There are many careers available that deal with electricity. Jobs such as an electrician can require four to five years working as an apprentice and attending trade school to become a journeyman. Electricians can find employment in a variety of fields, such as construction, building design, oil field work, and manufacturing plants. Journeymen electricians are in high demand across Canada and have the ability to earn very high salaries.

Electrical engineering is a profession that uses science, technology, and problem-solving skills to design, construct, and maintain products, services, and information systems. Electrical engineering is the historical name for what is now called electrical, electronics, and computer engineering. Electrical engineers require a bachelor's degree and are employable in numerous areas.

Careers that you might not think of that use electricity directly are actually very common. Paramedics, nurses, and other medical professionals make use of heart defibrillators. The defibrillator sends an electric shock to the heart to try and restore normal heart rhythm. RCMP officer's use a taser™ that sends an electric shock when they need to subdue an assailant. A small engine mechanic will come across electrical components in anything from a quad to a lawn mower. It is hard to think of a job that does not involve electricity in some form!

Practice

Use the following information to answer the next question.

> Susan researches career requirements on a government website. She notices that a particular career deals with the wiring of buildings and machines. This career requires knowledge of how electrical circuits operates well as electrical current.

27. The career that Susan is researching is **most likely**
    A. a mechanical engineer
    B. a computer scientist
    C. an electrician
    D. an architect

SOLUTIONS–PHYSICS: ELECTRICAL APPLICATIONS

1. D	7. C	13. B	19. OR	25. C
2. D	8. C	14. B	20. B	26. A
3. OR	9. OR	15. C	21. A	27. C
4. D	10. OR	16. C	22. C	
5. A	11. A	17. C	23. A	
6. OR	12. A	18. B	24. B	

1. D

Electrostatic force is the attractive or repulsive force between two charged particles. The friction between dry hair and the comb produces static electric charges on the comb. When the charged comb is brought near the neutral scraps of paper, it induces an opposite static charge on the scraps of paper. Consequently, the two opposite charges attract one another. Therefore, the scraps of paper were attracted toward the comb by an electrostatic force.

The comb and the scraps of paper are non-magnetic materials, so no magnetic force acts between them. Frictional force always opposes the relative movement of two bodies in contact, such as the comb and Nancy's hair. Since the comb and the scraps of paper are not in contact, frictional force does not act between the comb and the paper. A centripetal force any is force acting on a body that causes the body to rotate in a circular path. The comb and the scraps of paper are not rotating in circular paths, so there is no centripetal force acting between them.

2. D

The positively charged pesticide droplets induce a negative charge on the leaves, forming an electrostatic force between the droplets and the leaves. This electrostatic force attracts the drops to the leaves.

3. Open Response

Both the balloon and Kara's hair were initially neutral. That is, both had a balanced number of negative electrons and positive protons. When Kara rubbed the balloon on her hair, the force of friction caused the electrons from Kara's hair to travel to the balloon. The balloon became negatively charged.

The stream of running water was neutral. When the balloon was placed near the stream of water, the negatively charged particles in the balloon induced a positive charge in the stream of water, creating an attraction between the stationary balloon and the moving water.

4. D

The shock was caused by a buildup of static electricity; the resulting spark is called a discharge. Static electricity is the accumulation and storage of charged particles, resulting in a charged object. Touching something that is neutral or positively charged would result in an electrical discharge in the form of a spark and shock.

5. A

Balloon X was positively charged because it had five protons (+) and only three electrons (−). This means that balloon X had a positive charge.

The law of electrical charges states that "like charges repel." This means that a negative charge will repel another negative charge and a positive charge will repel another positive charge.

Therefore, in order for balloon Y to repel the positively charged balloon X, balloon Y also must have been positively charged. The only diagram that represents a positively charged balloon is diagram A, where the diagram shows six protons and three electrons for a total positive charge.

6. Open Response

Static electricity is the transfer of electrons from one object to another. When a charge stays in place for some length of time it is static electricity. In contrast, current electricity is the flow of charges within a circuit from an area of high energy to an area of low energy. Current electricity refers to the controlled flow of electric charges through a conductor. An electric circuit is a continuous, looping path, formed by a conductor, for electricity to flow through.

7. C

Adding more water to the tank increases the pressure. In the electrical analogy, pressure is referred to as voltage.

8. C

An analogy may be drawn between an electrical circuit and a water distribution system. In an electrical circuit, electrical charges flow through wires and in a water distribution system, water flows through pipes. Hence, electric charge is analogous to water.

9. Open Response

The change in the potential energy of the moving water as it falls from the top of the waterfall to the bottom represents the potential difference, or voltage, in an electrical circuit. The water flows with great speed and pressure through the narrow channel at the base of the waterfall. It then slows down as it enters into wider river bed. The rate of flow represents a high current and a low current, respectively. Current refers to the quantity of electrons and the rate with which they flow in a circuit.

The water movement is slowed down by the boulders. This is similar to the resistance created by tungsten wire in a light bulb.

10. Open Response

An ammeter measures the amount of electric current flowing in a circuit. To measure the electric current, an ammeter is connected directly into the part of the circuit for which the current is being measured. To connect the ammeter, disconnect an existing wire and connect the ammeter in series with the circuit.

11. A

The voltmeter needs to be placed in parallel over the load to measure the potential difference drop across it. The following diagram shows this placement:

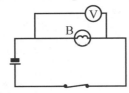

12. A

The current passing through Points S and T passes through one resistor. The current passing through Points U and V passes through two resistors. The more resistors a current passes through, the weaker the current becomes.

Resistance is lowest between points S and T in this circuit, meaning the current that flows through this point will be the highest compared with the rest of the circuit.

13. B

Jason used Ohm's Law, $V = R \times I$, to calculate the voltage passing through the light. The formula indicates that the resistance and current are directly proportional to the voltage. That means that an increase in the resistance will produce an increase in the voltage. It also means that an increase in the current will produce an increase in the voltage. When both the resistance and current are doubled, the voltage will increase 4 times (2×2). Therefore, the new voltage would be represented by the formula $V \times 4$.

14. B

The total resistance of the circuit is $R = R_1 + R_2 + r$

$= (4 + 20 + 1)\ \Omega = 25\ \Omega$.

Rearrange Ohm's law, $V = IR$, in order to solve for current.

$$I = \frac{V}{R}$$

$$I = \frac{1.5}{25} = 0.06 A$$

15. C

The efficiency in electrical devices is calculated using the formula $\frac{\text{output energy}}{\text{input energy}} \times 100$. Therefore, the ratio is multiplied by the value of 100.

16. C

The formula of efficiency:

$$\text{Efficiency} = \frac{\text{Output energy}}{\text{Input energy}} \times 100$$

Input energy to the generator = 12 000 J

Output energy from the generator = 6 800 J

Efficiency of the generator

$$= \left(\frac{6\ 800}{12\ 000} \times 100 \right)$$

$$= 56.7\%$$

17. C

In an electric appliance, a fuse will melt when a large current flows through it. As a result, the circuit switches off and the electric appliance is saved from damage. A ground wire connects the metallic casing of an electric appliance to Earth. This protects the device and the user from any static charge that may accumulate on the appliance's surface.

A transformer is a device that either increases or decreases voltage, as per output requirement. An ammeter measures the amount of current flowing through a circuit. Neither of these are safety devices.

A generator is a device that produces electrical energy. A voltmeter is a device that measures the potential drop across an appliance or an electrical circuit. Neither of these are safety devices.

A battery is a device that produces electrical energy, so it is not a safety device either.

18. B

All household electrical devices should be connected in parallel. If they were connected in series and one piece of equipment became defective, all the other appliance connected would also stop working.

19. **Open Response**

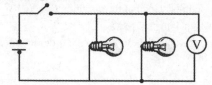

The voltmeter should be connected as shown to measure the current flowing through the outer lightbulb in the circuit.

20. **B**

In circuit I, the switches are connected in series. Closing one switch and leaving the other switch up leaves the circuit opened. This prevents the electricity from making a complete path. Because the current is interrupted, neither bulb will light up.

The switches and the bulbs in circuit II are connected in parallel. When the switch connected to one particular branch is closed, the current will pass through that branch only. Therefore, only the bulb connected in that branch will glow, so only one bulb will glow in circuit II in the given scenario.

21. **A**

A fuse is connected to a circuit in series. An overload in the circuit melts the fuse wire before the other conductors in the circuit become dangerously hot.

22. **C**

A fuse ⌇ should be inserted into the circuit.

A fuse is a metallic conductor that will melt from the heat of excessive current. The fuse will interrupt the current flow before the circuit wires heat up and burn.

23. **A**

Nuclear energy provides more energy per unit of fuel than other types of energy. This efficiency makes it less expensive over the long term, and easier on the environment.

24. **B**

The International Space Station has large solar panels that convert the sun's energy into electricity. Sunlight is readily available and is never obstructed in space.

25. **C**

When an electric current passes through an electric heater, the electrical energy changes into heat energy as it passes through the wire filament.

26. **A**

The operation of devices such as light bulbs, kettles, and heaters involves the passage of current through a filament. The heating effect of current in a filament is directly proportional to the resistance of the device. Therefore, devices such as electric bulbs, electric kettles, and electric heaters should have high resistances.

27. **C**

Electricians must know how electrical circuits and current electricity work. They also learn the best methods for wiring buildings and machines so that they operate safely and efficiently. Electricians must take courses specifically designed to help them learn the required courses. The required courses can most often be found online at company or government sites.

Use the following information to answer the next question.

According to the law of electrostatics, like charges _i_ each other and unlike charges _ii_ each other.

1. Which of the following tables completes the given statement?

   A.
i	ii
attract	repel

   B.
i	ii
attract	neutralize

   C.
i	ii
repel	attract

   D.
i	ii
neutralize	repel

2. Samuel's teacher asked him to demonstrate and explain the concept of static electricity to his class. When Samuel rubbed a balloon on his hair, the hair appeared to stick to the balloon. Samuel explained that friction created the static electricity and that the electrons

   A. changed in charge to become positive

   B. stopped moving from the hair to the balloon

   C. flowed continuous from the hair to the balloon

   D. built up in an area and moved in sudden bursts

3. Which of the following statements about water flow in a river is an analogy for electrical flow through a tungsten wire?

   A. A large rock in the river slows down the flow of water.

   B. The force of gravity causes the water to flow downhill.

   C. Water flows very quickly in the steep section of the stream.

   D. The volume of water flow is greatest in the wide part of the stream.

Use the following information to answer the next question.

An electrical metre was connected in-line to the components of the given circuit.

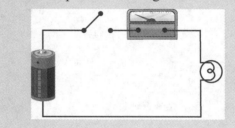

4. What kind of metre is shown in the given diagram?

   A. A voltmeter for measuring current

   B. An ammeter for measuring current

   C. A voltmeter for measuring resistance

   D. An ammeter for measuring resistance

*Use the following information to
answer the next question.*

Jasmine made an electrical circuit
consisting of a 12 V battery, light, rheostat,
ammeter, and voltmeter. She recorded the
current and voltage at various settings of
the rheostat.

Voltage (V)	Current (A)
2	0.02
4	0.04
6	0.06
8	0.08
10	0.10

5. Which of the following graphs shows the
relationship between the voltage and
current in Jasmine's experiment?

A.

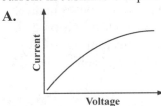

B.

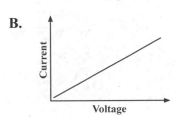

C.

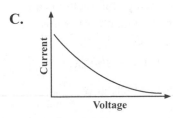

D.

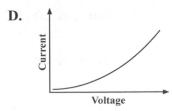

6. A 5 Ω resistor is connected in series with a
4 Ω resistor. If the measured flow of
current were 2.0 A, the potential difference
across the resistors would be

   A. 18 V   **B.** 19 V

   C. 20 V   **D.** 21 V

| Open Response |

7. A current of 3 A flows through a 15 Ω
resistor. What is the potential difference
across the resistor?

_____

_____

_____

_____

_____

*Use the following information to
answer the next question.*

An electric drill is supplied an input electric
energy of 1 000 J per second. The work
done by the drill is 400 J per second.

8. What is the percent efficiency of the
electric drill?

   A. 40   **B.** 50   **C.** 60   **D.** 70

Open Response

9. If a nuclear reactor produces 1 500 MW of useful energy with an efficiency of 30%, then what is the total energy input in the reactor?

_____

_____

_____

_____

_____

_____

_____

Use the following information to answer the next question.

Tia is concerned about electrical safety in her house. She hangs up a poster that illustrates four situations involving the use of electricity.

Electrical Safety

| Living room | Bedroom |
| Kitchen | Bathroom |

10. Which of the rooms on the poster shows a safe situation for dealing with electricity?

A. The kitchen   B. The bedroom

C. The bathroom   D. The living room

11. Which of the following statements **best** describes the wiring in a typical house?

A. The circuits in a house are wired in parallel and can have both lights and outlets on the same circuit.

B. The circuits in a house are wired in series and can have both lights and outlets on the same circuit.

C. The circuits in a house are wired in parallel and can have only lights or outlets on the same circuit.

D. The circuits in a house are wired in series and can have only lights or outlets on the same circuit.

Use the following information to answer the next question.

Bob observes that several houses in his neighbourhood have solar panels on their roofs. Bob's father tells him that using solar power has advantages and disadvantages.

12. Which of the following statements is an example of a disadvantage for using solar energy to produce electricity?

A. Solar power is non-polluting.

B. Solar power production is inconsistent.

C. Solar power is made from a renewable resource.

D. Solar power systems are inexpensive to maintain.

13. The operation of both an electric kettle and a light bulb is based on the

    A. heating effect of a current

    B. chemical effect of a current

    C. magnetic effect of a current

    D. piezoelectric effect of a current

Use the following information to answer the next question.

The given figure shows a circuit made of a battery and four bulbs, labelled I, II, III, and IV.

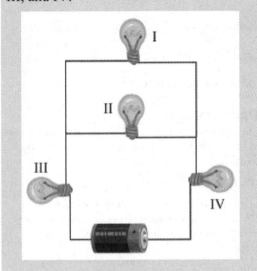

14. If bulb II and its wire connectors were removed from the circuit, then the current flowing through bulb I will

    A. remain unchanged

    B. decrease

    C. increase

    D. stop

SOLUTIONS

1. C	5. B	9. OR	13. A
2. D	6. A	10. A	14. C
3. A	7. OR	11. A	
4. B	8. A	12. B	

1. C

The fundamental law of electrostatics states that like charges repel each other and unlike charges attract each other.

2. D

In static electricity, the electrons build up and move in sudden bursts. Current electricity is the continuous flow of electrons through a conductor.

3. A

Tungsten wire has high resistance, so it slows down the flow of electrons. High resistance changes electrical energy into heat and light energy. The tungsten wire is analogous to a rock in a stream bed that slows down the flow of water.

4. B

A metre connected in-line as a substitute for the original connecting wires is an ammeter that measures current in the circuit. The current measured by the ammeter will be expressed in amperes or amps.

5. B

The points comparing the voltage and currents should be plotted in a straight line on the graph.

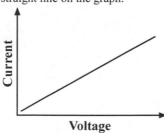

An increase in the voltage shows a direct increase in the current. The current is directly related to the voltage.

6. A

The circuit is arranged in series.
Total circuit resistance $(R) = 5 + 4 = 9\ \Omega$
Current flowing in the circuit $(I) = 2$ A
$$
\begin{aligned}
V &= IR \\
&= 2 \times 9 \\
&= 18 \text{ V}
\end{aligned}
$$

7. Open Response

Potential difference $V = IR$ where R is the resistance and I is the current.
The potential difference of the circuit is
$V = 3 \times 15 = 45$ V.

8. A

The formula for percent efficiency can be used to solve this problem.

$$\text{Percent efficiency} = \frac{\text{Output energy}}{\text{Input energy}} \times 100$$

$$= \frac{400}{1\ 000} \times 100 = 0.4 \times 100 = 40\%$$

The correct answer is A.

9. Open Response

The efficiency of a system is a ratio of the energy output of the system to the energy input, and can be calculated using the following equation.

$$\text{efficiency} = \frac{\text{energy output}}{\text{energy input}}$$

In this question, the energy output of the reactor is 1 500 MW and the reactor has an efficiency of 30%. The energy input can be calculated by rearranging the above equation:

$$\text{efficiency} = \frac{\text{energy output}}{\text{energy input}}$$

$$\text{energy input} = \frac{1\ 500 \text{ MV}}{0.30} = 5\ 000 \text{ MV}$$

It is important to note that the decimal equivalent of the efficiency is used in the equation in order to obtain the correct answer of 5 000 MW.

10. A

The toaster in the kitchen is unplugged while someone tries to fix it. Electrical appliances should always be disconnected from their power source when they are being repaired.

Having electricity close to water, such as the radio by the bathtub, is an unsafe use of electricity. Using electrical appliances with frayed wires is dangerous because it could cause the electricity to travel outside of the wire, starting a fire or electrocuting someone. Overloading a circuit, such as overloading a powerbar, is unsafe because it can cause the circuit to overheat and start a fire.

11. A

A typical house has circuits wired in parallel. When one light burns out the remaining lights and outlets on that circuit continue to work. A typical circuit usually has a combination of lights and outlets on one circuit.

12. B

Direct sunlight may not always be available, such as on cloudy days. As well, certain countries close to either the North or South poles receive drastically different amounts of sunlight in the different seasons. These areas receive very little sunlight during their winter months.

13. A

In both an electric kettle and an incandescent light bulb, current passes through a filament, causing it to heat up. Therefore, the operation of both is based on the heating effect of current.

14. C

The given circuit has bulbs I and II in a closed parallel circuit. In any parallel circuit, the total current is divided among each branch of the circuit. The currents flowing through bulbs I or II are less than those flowing through bulbs III or IV.

If bulb II were removed, then that branch will be opened, so no current will flow through it. The complete circuit will then be a closed series circuit, as represented in the following figure.

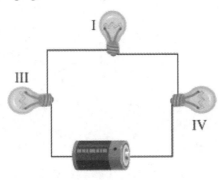

In this new circuit, the current flowing through bulbs I, III, and IV will be equal. If bulb II is removed from the circuit, then the current flowing through bulb I will increase.

Success on Tests

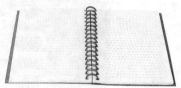

KEY STRATEGIES FOR SUCCESS ON TESTS

Things to Consider When Taking a Test

- It is normal to feel anxious before you write a test. You can manage this anxiety by:
    - thinking positive thoughts. Visual imagery is a helpful technique to try.
    - making a conscious effort to relax by taking several slow, controlled, deep breaths. Concentrate on the air going in and out of your body.
- Before you begin the test, ask questions if you are unsure of anything.
- Jot down key words or phrases from any oral directions.
- Look over the entire test to assess the number and kinds of questions on the test.
- Read each question closely and reread if necessary.
- Pay close attention to key vocabulary words. Sometimes these are bolded or italicized, and they are usually important words in the question.
- Mark your answers on your answer sheet carefully. If you wish to change an answer, erase the mark completely and then ensure your final answer is darker than the one you have erased.
- On the test booklet, use highlighting to note directions, key words, and vocabulary that you find confusing or that are important to answering the question.
- Double-check to make sure you have answered everything before handing in your test.

When taking tests, the easy words are often overlooked. Failure to pay close attention to these words can result in an incorrect answer. One way to avoid this is to be aware of these words and to underline, circle, or highlight these words while you are taking the test.

Even though some words are easy to understand, they can change the meaning of the entire question, so it is important that you pay attention to them. Here are some examples.

all	always	most likely	probably	best	not
difference	usually	except	most	unlikely	likely

Example

1. Which of the following items is **not** considered abiotic?
    A. Wind
    B. Bacteria
    C. Sunlight
    D. Precipitation

Helpful Strategies for Answering Multiple-Choice Questions

A multiple-choice question provides some information for you to consider and then asks you to select a response from four choices. Each question has one correct answer. The other answers are distractors, which are incorrect.

Below are some strategies to help you when answering multiple-choice questions.

- Quickly skim through the entire test. Find out how many questions there are and plan your time accordingly.

- Read and reread questions carefully. Underline key words and try to think of an answer before looking at the choices.

- If there is a graphic, look at the graphic, read the question, and go back to the graphic. Then, you may want to underline the important information from the question.

- Carefully read the choices. Read the question first and then each answer that goes with it.

- When choosing an answer, try to eliminate those choices that are clearly wrong or do not make sense.

- Some questions may ask you to select the best answer. These questions will always include words like **best**, **most appropriate**, or **most likely**. All of the answers will be correct to some degree, but one of the choices will be better than the others in some way. Carefully read all four choices before choosing the answer you think is the best.

- If you do not know the answer or if the question does not make sense to you, it is better to guess than to leave it blank.

- Do not spend too much time on any one question. Make a mark (*) beside a difficult question and come back to it. If you are leaving a question to come back to later, make sure you also leave the space on the answer sheet.

- Remember to go back to the difficult questions at the end of the test; sometimes clues are given throughout the test that will provide you with answers.

- Note any negative words like **no** or **not** and be sure your choice fits the question.

- Before changing an answer, *be sure* you have a very good reason to do so.

- Do not look for patterns on your answer sheet.

About Science Tests

What You Need to Know about Science Tests

To do well on a science test, you need to understand and apply your knowledge of scientific concepts. Reading skills can also make a difference in how well you perform. Reading skills can help you follow instructions and find key words, as well as read graphs, diagrams, and tables. Math skills are also important to success on science exams. Formulas are often used to solve scientific problems. Practicing with formulas is the best way to become good at them. They can also help you solve science problems.

Science tests usually have two types of questions: questions that ask for understanding of scientific concepts and questions that test how well you can solve scientific problems.

How You Can Prepare for the Science Test

Below are some strategies that are particular to preparing for and writing science tests.

- Know how to use your calculator and, if it is allowed, use your own for the test.

- Note-taking is a good way to review and study important information from your class notes and textbook.

- Sketch a picture of the problem, procedure, or term. Drawing is helpful for learning and remembering concepts.

- Check your answer to practice questions the require formulas by working backward to the beginning. You can find the beginning by going step-by-step in reverse order.

- When answering questions with graphics (pictures, diagrams, tables, or graphs), read the test question carefully.

  o Read the title of the graphic and any key words.

  o Read the test question carefully to figure out what information you need to find in the graphic.

  o Go back to the graphic to find the information you need.

- Always pay close attention when pressing the keys on your calculator. Repeat the procedure a second time to be sure you pressed the correct keys.

TEST PREPARATION COUNTDOWN

There is little doubt that if you develop a plan for studying and test preparation, you *will* perform well on tests.

Below is a general plan to follow seven days before you write a test.

Countdown: 7 Days before the Test

1. Use "Finding Out About the Test" to help you make your own personal test preparation plan.

2. Review the following information:

    • areas to be included on the test

    • types of test items

    • general and specific test tips

3. Start preparing for the test at least 7 days before the test. Develop your test preparation plan and set time aside to prepare and study.

Countdown: 6, 5, 4, 3, 2 Days before the Test

1. Review old homework assignments, quizzes, and tests.

2. Rework problems on quizzes and tests to make sure you still know how to solve them.

3. Correct any errors made on quizzes and tests.

4. Review key concepts, processes, formulas, and vocabulary.

5. Create practice test questions for yourself and then answer them. Work out many sample problems.

Countdown: The Night before the Test

6. The night before the test is for final preparation, which includes reviewing and gathering material needed for the test before going to bed.

7. Most important is getting a good night's rest and knowing you have done everything possible to do well on the test.

Test Day

8. Eat a healthy and nutritious breakfast.

9. Ensure you have all the necessary materials.

10. Think positive thoughts: "I can do this." "I am ready." "I know I can do well."

11. Arrive at your school early so you are not rushing, which can cause you anxiety and stress.

SUMMARY OF HOW TO BE SUCCESSFUL DURING THE TEST

The following are some strategies you may find useful for writing your test.

- Take two or three deep breaths to help you relax.

- Read the directions carefully and underline, circle, or highlight any important words.

- Survey the entire test to understand what you will need to do.

- Budget your time.

- Begin with an easy question or a question you know you can answer correctly rather than following the numerical question order of the test.

- If you cannot remember how to answer a question, try repeating the deep breathing and physical relaxation activities first. Then, move to visualization and positive self-talk to get you going.

- Write down anything you remember about the subject on the reverse side of your test paper. This activity sometimes helps you to remind yourself that you *do* know something and you *are* capable of writing the test.

- Look over your test when you have finished and double-check your answers to be sure you did not forget anything.

Practice Tests

Practice Tests

Table of Correlations

Specific Expectation		State Test 1	State Test 2
9.1.1	Understanding Basic Concepts		
9.1.1.1	describe the basic process of cell division, including what happens to the cell membrane and the contents of the nucleus	1	1
9.1.1.3	demonstrate an understanding that the nucleus of a cell contains genetic information and determines cellular processes	4	3, 4
9.1.1.4	describe various types of asexual reproduction that occur in plant species or in animal species and various methods for the asexual propagation of plants	5	5
9.1.1.5	describe the various types of sexual reproduction that occur in plants and in animals, and identify some plants and animals, including hermaphrodites, that exhibit this type of reproduction	6	6
9.1.1.6	compare sexual and asexual reproduction	7	7
9.1.1.7	explain signs of pregnancy in humans and describe the major stages of human development from conception to early infancy	8	8
9.1.1.2	demonstrate an understanding of the importance of cell division to the growth and reproduction of an organism	2, 3a, 3b	2
9.1.3	Relating Science to Technology, Society, and the Environment		
9.1.3.4	provide examples of the impact of developments in reproductive biology on global and local food production, populations, the spread of disease, and the environment		9
9.2.1	Understanding Basic Concepts		
9.2.1.1	describe an element as a pure substance made up of one type of particle or atom with its own distinct properties		10
9.2.1.3	describe compounds and elements in terms of molecules and atoms	11	12, 13
9.2.1.4	identify each of the three fundamental particles (neutron, proton, and electron), and its charge, location, and relative mass in a simple atomic model	12	14
9.2.1.5	identify general features of the periodic table	13, 14	15
9.2.1.6	demonstrate an understanding of the relationship between the properties of elements and their position in the periodic table	15	16
9.2.1.7	identify and write symbols/formulae for common elements and compounds	16	17
9.2.1.8	describe, using their observations, the evidence for chemical changes	17	18
9.2.1.9	distinguish between metals and nonmetals and identify their characteristic properties	18	19, 20
9.2.1.2	recognize compounds as pure substances that may be broken down into elements by chemical means	10	11
9.2.2	Developing Skills of Inquiry and Communication		
9.2.2.1a	"through investigations and applications of basic concepts: - demonstrate knowledge of laboratory, safety, and disposal procedures while conducting investigations"	19	
9.2.2.3	investigate the properties of changes in substances, and classify them as physical or chemical based on experiments		21
9.2.2.1b	- determine how the properties of substances influence their use	20	

	Specific Expectation	State Test 1	State Test 2
9.1.2	Developing Skills of Inquiry and Communication		
9.1.2.2	*use a microscope to observe and identify (in living tissue and prepared slides) animal and vegetable cells in different stages of mitosis, as well as cells undergoing asexual reproduction*	9	
9.3.1	Understanding Basic Concepts		
9.3.1.1	*recognize and describe the major components of the universe using appropriate scientific terminology and units*	21	22
9.3.1.3	*describe, compare, and contrast the general properties and motions of the components of the solar system*	23	25
9.3.1.4	*describe the sun and its effects on the Earth and its atmosphere*	24	26
9.3.1.5	*describe and explain the effects of the space environment on organisms and materials*	25, 26	27
9.3.1.2	*describe the generally accepted theory of the origin and evolution of the universe (i.e., the "big bang" theory) and the observational evidence that supports it*	22	23, 24
9.3.2	Developing Skills of Inquiry and Communication		
9.3.2.1a	*through investigations and applications of basic concepts: - identify problems and issues that scientists face when investigating celestial objects and describe ways these problems can be solved*		28
9.3.2.2	*conduct investigations on the motion of visible celestial objects, using instruments, tools, and apparatus safely, accurately, and effectively*	27	29
9.3.3	Relating Science to Technology, Society, and the Environment		
9.3.3.1	*identify and assess the impact of developments in space research and technology on other fields of endeavour*	28	30
9.3.3.3	*provide examples of the contributions of Canadian research and development to space exploration and technology*		32
9.3.3.2	*relate the beliefs of various cultures concerning celestial objects to aspects of their civilization*	29	31
9.4.1	Understanding Basic Concepts		
9.4.1.1	*explain common electrostatic phenomena*	30	33
9.4.1.3	*describe the concepts of electric current, potential difference, and resistance, with the help of a water analogy*	32	36
9.4.1.4	*explain how electric current, potential difference, and resistance are measured using an ammeter and a voltmeter*	33	37
9.4.1.5	*describe qualitatively the effects of varying electrical resistance and potential difference on electric current in an electrical circuit;*	34, 35	38
9.4.1.6	*apply the relationship potential difference = resistance × current resistance current to simple series circuits*	36	39
9.4.1.7	*determine quantitatively the percent efficiency of an electrical device that converts electrical energy to other forms of energy, using the relationship percent efficiency = $\frac{energy\ output}{energy\ input} \times 100$*	37	40
9.4.1.2	*compare qualitatively static and current electricity*	31	34, 35
9.4.2	Developing Skills of Inquiry and Communication		
9.4.2.2	*design, draw, and construct series and parallel circuits that perform a specific function*		43
9.4.2.1b	*- identify an authentic practical challenge or problem related to the use of electricity*	38	

Specific Expectation		State Test 1	State Test 2
9.4.3	Relating Science to Technology, Society, and the Environment		
9.4.3.1	*describe and explain household wiring and its typical components*		41
9.4.3.3	*compare electrical energy production technologies, including risks and benefits*		42
9.2.3	Relating Science to Technology, Society, and the Environment		

Practice Test 1

Ontario Science 9 Applied

1. The given images illustrate a sequence in cell division.

Which of the following images is the missing stage for the given sequence?

A.

B.

C.

D.

2. Mitosis is a type of cell division that aids all of the following functions **except**

   F. helping growth and cellular repair

   G. increasing the size of the organism

   H. maintaining the number of chromosomes

   J. reducing the number of chromosomes by half

3. There are two main types of cell division in living organisms. Cell division plays many roles during the life span of all organisms, including plants and animals.

Part A

Open Response

What is the main purpose for each of the two types of cell division: mitosis and meiosis?

_____

_____

_____

_____

_____

Part B

Open Response

Describe two roles of mitosis.

_____

_____

_____

_____

_____

_____

_____

_____

4. The nucleus is considered the brain of a cell because it regulates

   A. only the metabolic activities of the cell

   B. only the hereditary activities of the cell

   C. both the metabolic and hereditary activities of the cell

   D. both the hereditary and sensory perception activities of the cell

5. There are several types of asexual reproduction. They include binary fission, vegetative reproduction, and spore formation.

   Which of the following organisms reproduces through binary fission?

   F. Frog **G.** Coral

   H. Hydra **J.** Bacterium

6. In certain organisms, the male and female gametes from the same parent fuse to produce offspring.

   The described mode of reproduction is known as

   A. conjugation

   B. self-fertilization

   C. parthenogenesis

   D. cross-fertilization

7. What is the reason that asexual reproduction is generally a faster method of reproduction than sexual reproduction?

   F. Asexual reproduction does not require water and nutrients.

   G. Sexual reproduction does not require water and nutrients.

   H. Asexual reproduction does not require a mating partner.

   J. Sexual reproduction does not require a mating partner.

8. Fetal development follows embryonic development and is divided into three stages called

   A. zones **B.** periods

   C. quarters **D.** trimesters

9.

The division of a body cell.

The process of body cells dividing to create more body cells is called

F. fusion **G.** mating

H. mitosis **J.** meiosis

10. Which of the following statements about compounds is **not** true?

   A. A compound is homogeneous.

   B. No energy is involved in the formation of a compound.

   C. The components of a compound can be separated through chemical means.

   D. The properties of a compound are different from the properties of its components.

Go On

Ontario Science 9 Applied

11. Which of the following diagrams is a model of a molecule?

F.

G.

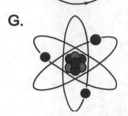

H.

J.

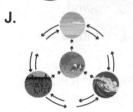

12. What are the three parts of an atom called?

A. Protons, photons, electrons

B. Protons, neutrons, photons

C. Electrons, photons neutrons

D. Electrons, neutrons, protons

13. What does the atomic number of an element indicate?

F. The number of electrons in an atom

G. The number of neutrons in an atom

H. The number of protons in an atom

J. The mass of an atom

14. How many elements are currently on the periodic table? How many of these are naturally occurring?

_____

_____

_____

_____

_____

15. Halogens should be placed into which group on the periodic table?

F. Group 2   G. Group 8

H. Group 14   J. Group 17

16. What is the chemical formula for ice?

A. O_2 B. He   C. CO_2 D. H_2O

17. Which of the following observations does **not** indicate a chemical change?

F. A solid forms within a solution.

G. Energy is released or taken in.

H. The substance changes colour.

J. Removing heat causes the change to reverse.

CHALLENGER QUESTION

18. Shruti was required to write observations for four substances displayed in her science class. The following chart shows some of the evidence she collected.

Substance	Evidence
1	Shiny, reddish solid; soft and bendable; conducts electricity
2	Grey-black solid; brittle; conducts electricity
3	Yellow, crumbly solid; does not conduct electricity
4	Dull, grey solid; bendable; conducts electricity

Which of the given substances are **most likely** non-metals?

A. 1 and 2   **B.** 1 and 4

C. 2 and 3   **D.** 3 and 4

19. According to modern electronic theory, the direction of current is indicated by the flow of the

F. conventional current

G. positive charges

H. electrons

J. protons

20. Which of the following elements is a good conductor of heat and electricity?

A. Zinc   **B.** Carbon

C. Fluorine   **D.** Calcium

21. Which of the following celestial bodies are described by shapes such as spiral, barred, and elliptical?

F. Galaxies   **G.** Nebulae

H. Planets   **J.** Stars

22. One piece of evidence that supports the big bang theory is the redshift of stars, which results from stars' movements away from each other. As a result of the increasing distances between stars, the wavelengths of light travelling from the stars toward Earth shift toward the higher wavelength, which is red light.

The redshift of stars occurs as a result of the

A. expansion of the universe

B. magnetic repulsion of the stars

C. explosions taking place in space

D. gravitational pull of other heavenly objects

23. Which two planets in the solar system have an asteroid belt between them?

F. Mars and Jupiter

G. Venus and Earth

H. Jupiter and Earth

J. Saturn and Uranus

24. Which of the following types of radiation causes the greenhouse effect?

A. Light rays

B. Microwaves

C. Infrared radiation

D. Ultraviolet radiation

Go On

Ontario Science 9 Applied

25. Astronauts are exposed to microgravity in space, which means that they are subjected to

F. slightly greater gravity than on Earth

G. much greater gravity than on Earth

H. slightly less gravity than on Earth

J. much less gravity than on Earth

Open Response

26. List four hazards associated with survival in space.

_____

_____

_____

_____

_____

_____

_____

_____

27.

The time of day indicated by the sundial in the given picture is

F. early morning   **G.** late evening

H. afternoon   **J.** noon

28. There are many common technologies now used that were originally developed for use in space. Which of the following devices used by firefighters developed from a technology originally intended for space exploration?

A. Fire hose

B. Fire extinguisher

C. Fire-resistant suit

D. Firefighter's helmet

29. According to historic descriptions, which of the following celestial bodies shine like "hairy stars" when they pass near the sun?

F. Planets   **G.** Comets

H. Asteroids   **J.** Meteorites

30. Which of the following situations is an example of static charge?

A. A doorbell rings when the button is pressed.

B. The filament in a toaster gets hot when the knob switch is pushed down.

C. Pieces of paper are attracted to a glass rod that has been rubbed in flannel.

D. A thermostat switches on the furnace motor when the room temperature drops.

31. Electric current is the

F. continuous flow of charge in a definite direction

G. continuous flow of charge in random directions

H. random arrangement of charge

J. rate of flow of the charge

32. In a water distribution system, water flows through tubes and pipes because of the pressure gradient, or pressure difference.

    If a water distribution system is an analogy for an electric circuit, the pressure gradient of the water distribution system would be the
    A. electric charge in an electric circuit

    B. electric current in an electric circuit

    C. circuit resistance in an electric circuit

    D. potential difference in an electric circuit

33. A galvanometer is an instrument that uses a magnetic needle in an electrical field to detect small currents of electricity.

    In order to measure the electric current in a circuit, a galvanometer is connected
    F. in series to the circuit

    G. in parallel to the circuit

    H. at any point in the circuit

    J. near the cell in the circuit

34. The students of Century Junior High School entered a competition to design the fastest electric-powered car at the Science Olympics fair. One of the entries in the competition was a design with a battery operated car with a motor attached to the wheels. What would happen if a resistor were added to the circuit between the battery and the motor of this car?
    A. The motor will run faster.

    B. The motor will run slower.

    C. The wires will become hot.

    D. The voltage in the circuit will increase.

Open Response

35. Kelly was given a package of two D-cell batteries, wire connectors, a switch, a 5 ohm resistor, and a 10 ohm resistor. She was asked to make a circuit with the brightest light using the components from the package. Explain how Kelly would construct an electrical circuit that would provide the greatest intensity of light.

    _____

    _____

    _____

    _____

    _____

36.

    In the given circuit, three resistors of 2 Ω, 4 Ω, and R Ω, are connected to a 2 V battery with an internal resistance of 3 Ω. A main current of 0.25 A flows through the circuit.

    What is the potential difference across the internal resistance of the battery?
    A. 0.25 volts   B. 0.50 volts

    C. 0.75 volts   D. 1.25 volts

37. If 2 000 J of energy were provided to an electric engine with an efficiency of 30%, then the output energy of the engine would be
    F. 200 J   G. 400 J

    H. 600 J   J. 800 J

Go On

38. Many schools have decided to use fluorescent light bulbs instead of incandescent ones. Which of the following statements explains the reason that fluorescent lights are more efficient than incandescent lights?

A. Fluorescent lights use less electricity than incandescent bulbs and give off less heat.

B. Fluorescent lights use more electricity than incandescent bulbs and give off more heat.

C. Fluorescent lights use the same amount of electricity as incandescent bulbs and produce less heat.

D. Fluorescent lights use the same amount of electricity as incandescent bulbs and give off large amounts of heat.

Practice Test 2

Ontario Science 9 Applied

1. Meiotic cell division takes place during fertilization, whereas the cell division that occurs in cleavage is
   A. mitotic
   B. amitotic
   C. mitotic and amitotic
   D. meiotic and amitotic

2. There are three distinct phases in the life cycle of a cell: interphase, mitosis, and cytokinesis. Each phase has its own special characteristics. Which of the following lists describes the order in which mitosis occurs?
   F. Prophase → metaphase → anaphase → telophase
   G. Telophase → metaphase → anaphase → prophase
   H. Prophase → telophase → metaphase → anaphase
   J. Anaphase → metaphase → telophase → prophase

3. In which part of the cell is genetic material contained?
   A. The cell mitochondria
   B. The cell membrane
   C. The cell vacuoles
   D. The cell nucleus

   Open Response

4. What is the function of a nucleus in a cell?
   _____
   _____
   _____
   _____
   _____

5. Strawberry plants can produce new plants at the end of their stems. These new developments are called runners. The type of asexual reproduction shown by strawberry plants is referred to as
   A. fission
   B. budding
   C. spore formation
   D. vegetative propagation

6. Hermaphrodites are organisms that possess both male and female reproductive organs. They can reproduce through self-fertilization and cross-fertilization.

   Which of the following organisms reproduces through self-fertilization?
   F. Tapeworm   G. Earthworm
   H. Hamlets   J. Leech

7. An important difference between sexual and asexual reproduction is that asexual reproduction typically
   A. produces more variety among the offspring
   B. produces offspring through a slower process
   C. results in a relatively rapid production of offspring
   D. results in the production of relatively few offspring

8. When can the organ systems and nerves first be identified during the development of human offspring?
   F. Blastula stage   G. First trimester
   H. Third trimester   J. Second trimester

9. The development of a disease-resistant canola plant has resulted in improved crop yields for prairie farmers.

The technique used to develop disease-resistant canola varieties is known as

A. cloning

B. *in vitro* fertilization

C. genetic engineering

D. artificial insemination

10. Many metals are pure elements, which means that they are

F. made of expensive metals

G. made up of one kind of atom

H. made by a chemical reaction

J. made of one kind of molecule

11. If the components of a substance cannot be separated physically, the substance is

A. a mixture

B. a compound

C. a pure substance

D. an impure substance

12. Which of the following statements about compounds and elements is **false**?

F. Elements can be combined to form a compound.

G. The elements present in a compound can be separated.

H. The properties of compounds are the same as elements.

J. A compound is a substance that contains two or more elements.

Open Response

13. The universe is composed of all matter. Matter includes pure substances made up of elements and compounds.

What is the difference between an element and a compound?

_____

_____

_____

_____

_____

14. An atom consists of a nucleus in its centre and a negatively charged cloud of matter that orbits around the nucleus.

What particles make up the nucleus of an atom?

F. Protons

G. Electrons

H. Neutrons and protons

J. Protons and electrons

Go On

15. In the long form of the periodic table, the elements that have similar properties
    A. recur after every three elements
    B. recur after every eight elements
    C. form horizontal rows
    D. form vertical groups

16. Noble gases are elements that have a low level of reactivity. As a result of this characteristic, these gases are referred to as inert gases.

    Which group on the periodic table contains the noble gases?
    F. Group 1   G. Group 6
    H. Group 17   J. Group 18

17. Salt is a mineral essential for animal and human life. Salt is produced in different forms, such as sea salt, refined table salt, and iodized salt. Salt is a hard brittle crystal that can be white, pink, or light gray in colour.

    Which two elements make up the compound **most commonly** known as table salt?
    A. Carbon and oxygen
    B. Sodium and chlorine
    C. Hydrogen and oxygen
    D. Manganese and sodium

18. A student reads the following four observations in a friend's science journal:
    - **Observation 1** The egg white changed from clear to white as it was fried.
    - **Observation 2** The wet steel wool turned a reddish colour when exposed to air.
    - **Observation 3** The salt dissolved quickly when it was stirred in water.
    - **Observation 4** The candle flame gave off heat.

    All of the above described chemical reactions, **except** for which observation?
    F. Observation 1   G. Observation 2
    H. Observation 3   J. Observation 4

19. Electrical wires are made from metals because
    A. electricity can easily pass through metals
    B. electricity cannot pass through metals
    C. metals do not heat quickly
    D. metals can be bent easily

    | Open Response |

20. What is the reason that copper is considered a good conductor of electricity?

    _____
    _____
    _____
    _____
    _____

21. Which of the following properties is characteristic of a physical change?
    A. The change is irreversible.

    B. No new substance formed.

    C. Does not need a supply of energy.

    D. The mass of substance remains fixed.

22. Measuring time and distance in space is different than measuring it on Earth. Distances and time spans are much greater in space than those used for measuring on Earth.

    Which of the following distances is **least likely** measured in light years?
    F. The distance between the sun and the planets in the solar system

    G. The distance between two points on a planet

    H. The distance between stars and galaxies

    J. The distance between two planets

23. The star Alpha Centauri is the star closest to Earth other than the sun, and it is moving away from Earth. Astronomers know that Alpha Centauri is moving away from Earth because the wavelength of its light is becoming __i__ and the colour band for its light is shifting to the __ii__ end of the spectrum.

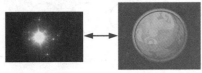

Which of the following tables contains the information that completes the given statement?

A.

i	ii
stretched out	blue

B.

i	ii
stretched out	red

C.

i	ii
compressed	blue

D.

i	ii
compressed	red

Open Response

24. What observation caused scientists to develop a theory about the expansion of the universe?

_____

_____

_____

_____

_____

Go On ▶

Ontario Science 9 Applied

25. The given diagram shows the path of a comet within the solar system. The ellipse is the comets path, and objects A–E are the relative positions of the sun and the four planets closest to the sun.

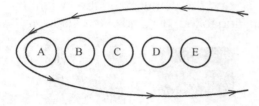

At which position should Earth be located?

A. A   **B.** B   **C.** C   **D.** D

26. A telescopic view of the sun's surface shows dark areas that appear to be at a lower temperature than the rest of the surface. What is the scientific term that describes these dark areas?

F. Sunspots   **G.** Black holes

H. Dark matter   **J.** Sun patches

27. As a result of zero gravity, crew members aboard spacecraft experience weightlessness.

Weightlessness causes physical complications that may include all of the following conditions **except**

A. anemia

B. blocked sinuses

C. extra weight gain

D. loss of bone tissue

28. Space junk is a term used for floating debris that orbits Earth. What is the reason that space junk could be a danger to space travel?

F. Astronauts have a hard time bringing it home to recycle.

G. It pollutes the atmosphere, reducing visibility for astronauts.

H. It can block the sun, leaving no source of heat for astronauts.

J. It could hit and damage the spacecraft used to travel in space.

Open Response

29. James wants to conduct an experiment to determine the cause of a peculiar rash that appears when a person is exposed to Brand X deodorant. He knows that keeping accurate data records when conducting this experiment is important. James writes four statements that he believes are important for keeping accurate data in any experiment.

Statement 1: Accurate data records are required to determine whether the prediction is true.
Statement 2: Accurate data records will help ensure that no one else conducts the same experiment.
Statement 3: Accurate data records will help other scientists replicate and validate the results.
Statement 4: Accurate data records ensure that the test sample used should be smaller in size.

Explain which of James's four statements are valid for explaining the importance for keeping accurate data in an experiment.

_____
_____
_____
_____
_____

30. Technology developed for space has also had an impact on Earth. Many different technologies used in space can be adapted to serve different purposes on Earth.

How has the technology used for space shuttle fuel pumps helped society?

F. It has made oil extraction safer.

G. It has helped develop better artificial hearts.

H. It helped to develop better navigational aids.

J. It has brought us higher quality satellite signals.

31. According to some Aboriginal stories, people used to hunt and work only during the daytime because there was no light during the night. According to these stories, the problem of being able to see at night was solved by the creation of

A. stars

B. meteors

C. the moon

D. the Northern Lights

32. The Canadarm has performed all of the following functions **except** for

F. launching satellites

G. gathering samples from asteroids

H. assisting to dock the space shuttle

J. fixing the Hubble Space Telescope

Go On ▶

33. When removing a load of clothes from her clothes dryer, Tia noticed that all her sweaters were stuck together. She concluded that this was an example of

A. static electricity produced by like charges

B. static electricity produced by unlike charges

C. current electricity produced by neutral objects

D. current electricity produced by the conducting clothes

34. Leanne told her science partner that electrical energy causes both the electroscope and compact disc player to work. In an electroscope, __i__ electricity causes the foil strips move apart, while __ii__ electricity causes the motor to turn the disc in the disk player.

Which of the following tables contains the information that completes the given statement?

F.

i	ii
current	static

G.

i	ii
static	static

H.

i	ii
static	current

J.

i	ii
current	current

| Open Response |

35. Which type of electricity, current or static, is used to create electrical power? What is the reason that this type of electricity is used?

_____

_____

_____

_____

_____

36. Water flowing down a small stream is slowed down by a beaver dam. Which electrical concept is **best** described by this water analogy?

F. Power   G. Voltage

H. Current   J. Resistance

37. Which of the following circuit diagrams shows the correct placement of a voltmeter for measuring the electric potential energy across lamp A?

A.

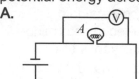

B.

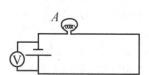

C.

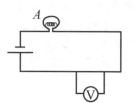

D.

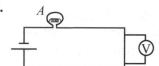

38. Sheldon built a circuit using the given circuit schematic.

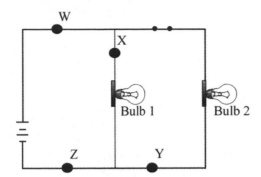

At which point on the diagram should Sheldon place a resistor in order to reduce the brightness of bulb 2 without affecting bulb 1?

F. W   **G.** X   **H.** Y   **J.** Z

39. A current of I amperes flows through a circuit with a resistor of R ohms. What is the potential difference across the resistor?

A. $I^2 R$

B. $\dfrac{I}{R}$

C. IR

D. $\dfrac{R}{I}$

40. The useful energy output of an iron for the time it takes Leroy to iron his white shirt for his middle school jazz band is 1 850 kJ. The total energy input for this period of time is 2 250 kJ.

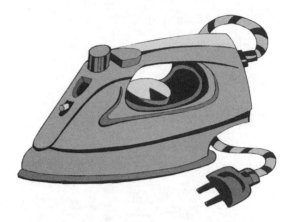

What is the energy efficiency of Leroy's iron over this period of time?

F. 0.82%   **G.** 1.22%

H. 82%   **J.** 122%

41. Electricity enters into your house through an underground cable. An electrician uses this power source to build a circuit required for each room.

Which of the following lists shows the correct sequence of components an electrician would use to construct a simple circuit for a bedroom?

A. Source, outlet, circuit breaker, light

B. Source, light, outlet, circuit breaker

C. Source, circuit breaker, outlet, light

D. Source, light, circuit breaker, outlet

Go On ▶

42. Tides and waves are very important natural energy resources. The use of energy from tides and waves has resulted in an increase in

F. electrical power production

G. fish population

H. water pollution

J. water travel

43. A student set up this circuit.

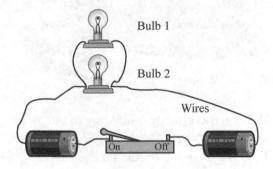

What would the student **most likely** predict if bulb 2 were removed from the circuit?

A. The batteries would overheat.

B. The wires would short circuit.

C. Bulb 1 would remain lit.

D. Bulb 1 would go out.

SOLUTIONS–PRACTICE TEST 1

1. **B**	8. **D**	16. **D**	24. **C**	32. **D**
2. **J**	9. **H**	17. **J**	25. **J**	33. **F**
3. Part A- **OR**	10. **B**	18. **C**	26. **OR**	34. **B**
Part B- **OR**	11. **H**	19. **H**	27. **F**	35. **OR**
4. **C**	12. **D**	20. **A**	28. **C**	36. **C**
5. **J**	13. **H**	21. **F**	29. **G**	37. **H**
6. **B**	14. **OR**	22. **A**	30. **C**	38. **A**
7. **H**	15. **J**	23. **F**	31. **F**	

1. B

Examine the given stages and the structure of chromosomes carefully. Since the genetic material is in the form of chromatids, rather than as homologous chromosomes, the sequence represents meiosis II. The pictures show prophase I, the unknown phase, anaphase I, and telophase I. The missing stage is metaphase II, which is shown in B.

Figure A represents crossing-over in prophase I.

Figure C represents anaphase I when the two homologous chromosomes separate.

Figure D represents metaphase I of meiosis I when the homologous chromosomes arrange on the equatorial plate the cell.

2. J

Mitosis is a type of cell division that maintains the number of chromosomes in the next generation, helps in growth and cellular repair, and causes the organism to increase in size. It is not responsible for reducing the number of chromosomes to half. In meiotic division, the chromosomal number is reduced to half.

3. Part A – Open Response

Mitosis is the cell division in which two new genetically identical cells are produced.

Meiosis is the cell division in which reproductive cells are produced. They contain half the genetic information of the parent cell.

Part B – Open Response

Two roles of mitosis are growth and repair. Growth and repair can also include these types of discussions:

• Growth of a child (from a baby to an adult)
• Repairing damaged tissues after an accident
• Growth of a new individual (from one cell to a baby)
• Replacing cells from tissues that do not live forever (skin cells, blood cells, stomach lining)

4. C

The nucleus is described as the brain of a cell because it regulates both the metabolic and hereditary activities.

5. J

Asexual reproduction occurs in most single-celled organisms, although some plants also reproduce asexually. Binary fission is a form of asexual reproduction in which a cell divides to produce cells of equal, or nearly equal, size. Bacteria reproduce through binary fission.

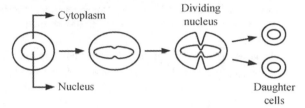

Frogs reproduce sexually. Frogs do not reproduce through binary fission.

Corals mainly reproduce sexually, but they can also reproduce asexually by budding. However, corals do not reproduce through binary fission.

Hydras reproduce asexually by the process of budding. They can also reproduce sexually, although this is less common. Hydras do not reproduce through binary fission.

6. B

Self-fertilization is characterized by the fusion of male and female gametes from the same parent.

7. H

Asexual reproduction is usually a faster method of reproduction because there is no need to find a mating partner in order to reproduce. Asexual reproduction involves the production of offspring from a single organism.

8. D

Fetal development is divided into three stages called trimesters. These take place over approximately 38 weeks in humans.

9. H

The process for making more body cells in order to grow and repair the body involves the creation of daughter cells. Cell division that leads to identical daughter cells is called mitosis.

Meiosis describes a special form of cell division in which the resulting cells have fewer chromosomes than the parent. Mating describes sexual reproduction, and fusion is the process whereby two cells fuse or combine. There are few, if any, examples of fusion happening with normal animal or plant cells.

10. B

The formation of a compound requires energy.

11. H

Molecules cannot be seen without the use of a microscope. Scientists have developed models so you can see what a molecule looks like and how the pieces of a molecule fit together. Diagram H is a model of a water molecule. It is made up of one large oxygen atom, and two smaller hydrogen atoms.

Diagram F is a model of the solar system. Diagram G is a model of an atom. Diagram J is a model of the water cycle.

12. D

Atoms are made up of electrons, neutrons, and protons. At the centre of the atom is the nucleus. The nucleus contains protons, which have a positive charge, and neutrons, which have no charge. Circling the nucleus are the electrons, which have a negative charge.

13. H

The atomic number is the number of protons contained in the nucleus of an atom. A common mistake is to assume that the atomic number also conveys the number of electrons in an atom. This is only true for the non-ionized form of the atom. Ions have a different number of electrons than protons, resulting in a net positive or negative charge.

For example, chlorine (Cl) has an atomic number of 17, and it has 17 electrons in its non-ionized form. However, chlorine has 18 electrons when it is an ion (Cl^-), while both the ionized form and the non-ionized form have 17 protons. The mass of an atom is equal to the number of protons plus the number of neutrons.

14. Open Response

There are currently 117 elements in the periodic table. Of these, 93 naturally occur on Earth.

15. J

Halogens are a series of non-metal elements; they are placed in Group 17 on the periodic table.

Group 2 of the periodic table contains the alkaline earth metals. Group 8 contains the transition metals. Group 14 contains the elements of the carbon family.

16. D

Ice is a solid form of water. The formula for water is H_2O. Therefore, the formula for ice is also H_2O.

17. J

A chemical change is not easily reversible, so if the change can be reversed by removing heat, it is most likely a physical change. By adding heat to liquid water, it is possible to make it evaporate. By removing the heat, the vapour changes back to liquid water. These are physical changes, not chemical changes.

18. C

Non-metals are not good conductors of electricity and are crumbly solids or brittle. So substances 2 and 3 are most likely non-metals.

19. H

According to modern electronic theory, the direction of the electric current is indicated by the flow of negatively charged electrons, which flows in the opposite direction to the conventional current.

20. A

Metals, like zinc, are good conductors of heat and electricity. The other alternatives are elements that are not metals.

21. F

Galaxies have different shapes, including spiral, barred, and elliptical. For example, the Andromeda galaxy is spiral in shape, while the Milky Way galaxy, home to Earth's solar system, is considered to be barred and spiral in shape.

22. A

Stars are moving away from each other as a result of the expansion of the universe. This supports the big bang theory, which states that the universe has come to its present condition because it expanded from its primordial condition and is still expanding.

Distractor Rationale

B. The magnetic force acting between stars and Earth is very weak. The movement of stars away from each other does not occur because of magnetic repulsion.

C. The movement of stars away from each other does not occur because of explosions in space.

D. Since gravitational pull always attracts two objects toward each other, stars cannot move away from each other as a result of gravitational pull.

23. F

The asteroid belt is found between Mars and Jupiter.

24. C

When visible light falls on an object, it transfers its energy to that object. The object is heated by this transferred energy, and it radiates this energy as infrared (IR) radiation as it cools down. Infrared radiation has longer wavelengths than visible light, so the glass of the greenhouse allows visible light to pass through but stops the infrared radiation. This traps the heat inside the greenhouse. The same situation occurs when short wavelength radiation from the sun enters through Earth's atmosphere. Earth radiates heat energy with longer wavelengths that cannot penetrate through the atmosphere, so the heat is reflected back to the surface.

25. J

Astronauts in space are exposed to microgravity because of their distance from earth. The force of gravity is significantly lower, and therefore they experience the phenomenon of weightlessness while in space

26. Open Response

The following is a list of some of the hazards associated with survival in space. Students may find other hazards.
1. Psychological problems associated with being confined in a small space
2. Dangers associated with floating space junk
3. Problems associated with weightlessness
4. Exposure to high levels of radiation
5. Physical strain on the body

27. F

The shadow of the sundial is on the western side of the dial and its length is long. Since the sun rises in the east, the sundial indicates a time in the early morning.
The shadow of the sundial in the late afternoon would be on the eastern side of the dial. The shadow of the sundial the late afternoon would be at the eastern side of the dial. The shadow of the sundial at noon would be on the middle of the dial and its length would be short

28. C

Fire-resistant suits developed from a technology originally intended for space exploration.

29. G

Due to their physical appearance as they approach the sun, comets were known as "hairy stars."

30. C

Pieces of paper are attracted to a glass rod that has been rubbed in flannel due to static charge.

31. F

Electric current is defined as the continuous flow of charge in a definite direction. If two insulated conductors are at different potentials and are connected by a wire, the positive charge will flow from the higher potential to the lower potential, and the negative charge will flow from lower to higher.

32. D

An analogy may be drawn between an electrical circuit and a water distribution system. In a water distribution system, water flows through tubes and pipes because of the pressure gradient, or pressure difference. In an electrical circuit, electric current flows through wires as a result of potential difference. Therefore, the pressure difference is analogous to potential difference.

33. F

Both the ammeter and the galvanometer work when an electrical current deflects a magnetic needle. The ammeter measures a large current, while the galvanometer measures a small current. In either case, the instruments are connected in series into the existing circuit.

34. B

A resistor takes away some of the electrical energy supplied by the battery. As a result, there is less energy to run the motor. The motor will slow down.

35. Open Response

Kelly needs to make a circuit that has the most current passing through it with the least resistance for that current. She could use the two D cells to provide the most voltage for the light. Kelly would not use either of the resistors. Resistors use up energy, resulting in less current for the light.
Kelly's circuit would include two D cells, one light, and a switch.

36. C

The potential difference across 3 Ω (the internal resistance of the battery)
$= R \times I$
$= 3 \times 0.25$
$= 0.75$ V

Therefore, the potential difference across the battery is 0.75 V.

37. H

This problem can be solved by using the formula for percent efficiency,

$$\text{Percent efficiency} = \frac{\text{Output energy}}{\text{Input energy}} \times 100$$

$$\Rightarrow \text{Output energy} = \frac{\text{Percent efficiency}}{100} \times \text{Input energy}$$

$$\Rightarrow \frac{30}{100} \times 2\ 000 = 600 \text{ J}$$

38. **A**
   Fluorescent lights use less electricity, and give off less heat
   than incandescent bulbs. This makes them more efficient
   and helps reduce the amount of electricity used by
   buildings and the overall cost for power.

SOLUTIONS–PRACTICE TEST 2

1. A	10. G	19. A	28. J	37. A
2. F	11. B	20. OR	29. OR	38. H
3. D	12. H	21. B	30. G	39. C
4. OR	13. OR	22. G	31. C	40. H
5. D	14. H	23. B	32. G	41. C
6. F	15. D	24. OR	33. B	42. F
7. C	16. J	25. D	34. H	43. C
8. G	17. B	26. F	35. OR	
9. C	18. H	27. C	36. J	

1. A

Cleavage involves a series of mitotic divisions that gives rise to daughter cells that are genetically similar to the parent cell. This increase in the number of cells ultimately forms a solid mass called the *morula*. This development occurs by mitosis.

2. F

The correct order in which mitosis happens is Prophase → metaphase → anaphase → telophase.

3. D

The genetic material of a cell is contained in the cell nucleus.

4. Open Response

The nucleus is the brain or decision maker of the cell. It controls the growth and development of each cell and controls all the activity of the cell parts. The nucleus has a master set of instructions that determines what job a cell will perform and how each cell will grow and divide. The instructions are carried on two molecules of DNA.

5. D

Vegetative propagation is the method of asexual reproduction by which strawberry plants form runners. A creeping stem with long internodes that run horizontally on the surface of the soil is called a runner. Roots are given out at nodes, and auxiliary buds form new aerial shoots.

Fission, budding, and spore formation are methods of asexual reproduction seen in organisms such as amoebas, fungi, and hydras.

6. F

The tapeworm is a hermaphrodite that reproduces through the process of self-fertilization.

7. C

Asexual reproduction often results in the rapid production of a large number of offspring, whereas sexual reproduction usually results in a comparatively less rapid increase in number.

8. G

Organs and systems and nerves can be identified by week twelve, the end of the first trimester.

9. C

Genetic engineering has allowed scientists to develop disease-resistant canola plants and improved the crop yields for prairie farmers. Plants can now be genetically engineered to be resistant to various pests as well, allowing more of the crops to be used.

10. G

Pure elements are made up of one kind of atom. Aluminium, iron, nickel, copper, silver, and gold are all pure element metals.

11. B

Compounds are composed of two or more elements, which cannot be separated by physical means.

12. H

Elements and compounds have different properties. Elements are made of only one kind of atom. Compounds are formed by combining the atoms from two or more elements. Silver is an example of an element that is made from one type of atom. Carbon dioxide is an example of a compound because it is made up of the elements oxygen and carbon.

13. Open Response

Elements are composed of one kind of atom and cannot be broken down any further. A compound is a substance that is composed of the atoms from two or more different elements that have chemically combined together. Compounds can be broken down into their elements by chemical means.

14. H

The nucleus of an atom contains both protons and neutrons, while the electrons orbit the nucleus in the form of charged clouds. Electrons are not present in the nucleus of an atom.

15. D

The modern periodic table is known as the long form of the periodic table. The elements in the modern periodic table are arranged in the increasing order of their atomic numbers. In this table, the elements that have similar properties are present in vertical groups as the electronic configuration of elements present in these groups is similar.

16. J

Group 18 on the periodic table contains the noble gases. Group 1 on the periodic table contains the alkali metals. Group 6 on the periodic table contains the transition metals. Group 17 on the periodic table contains the halogens.

17. B

Salt is primarily composed of the elements sodium and chlorine and is commonly known as sodium chloride. A molecule of salt contains one sodium atom and one chlorine atom. It is produced mainly from the evaporation of seawater.

18. H

Here, you need to know that there are clues to help scientists determine if a chemical reaction has occurred. In observations 1, 2, and 4, chemical reactions have occurred. The egg changed colour and composition as it cooked. The steel wool changed colour as it rusted. The candle flame gave off heat. In observation 3, there was no chemical reaction when the salt mixed with the water. The salt dissolved, which is a physical change.

19. A

Electric wires are made from metals because electricity can pass very easily through metals. This means they are good conductors of electricity.

Metals are good conductors of heat, which causes them to heat up quickly. However, because wires are typically covered in insulators such as rubber or plastic, they do not lose much heat to their surroundings. Some metals, like copper and aluminium, can be bent easily, but this is not true of all metals.

20. Open Response

Objects through which electricity can pass easily are called good conductors of electricity. All electrical wires are made of metal because most metals are good conductors. Copper is inexpensive, durable, and allows electric currents to pass through it very easily. Therefore, almost all electrical wires are made of copper. Copper wire is also considered safer than aluminium wiring, which is another reason it is preferred.

21. B

A physical change is a temporary change and does not involve the formation of a new substance.

22. G

The distance between two points on a planet could be measured in kilometres, whereas the other distances would be too large to measure in anything other than light years.

23. B

Scientists can tell that Alpha Centauri is moving away from Earth because the wavelength of its light is becoming stretched out and the colour band for its light is shifting to the red end of the spectrum. This redshift of the colour band occurs when a light source moves away from an observer.

24. Open Response

While observing the nature and characteristics of galaxies in the universe, scientists found that some galaxies are moving away from each other at extremely high speeds, almost as fast as the speed of light. Movement at such high speed could only be possible with the sudden availability of enormous space. Scientists believed this space could only be made available as a result of expansion of the universe, which led them to develop a theory pertaining to this.

25. D

Comets orbit around our Sun due to the Sun's powerful gravitational pull. Because the Sun has more gravitational pull than any other planet or object in our solar system the comet circles it and passes back out in to deep space. This information indicates that A should be the position for the Sun. Given the positions of the planets, then position B = Mercury, position C = Venus, position D = Earth, and position E = Mars. Most scientists think comets come from the Oort cloud, a spherical region of dust clouds that surrounds our solar system.

26. F

These dark areas that appear to be at a lower temperature are referred to as sunspots. Solar flares from the sun usually occur around sunspots.

27. C

Weightlessness due to the effect of microgravity causes many complications but not extra weight gain. Bones and muscles will experience less pressure, so they will expand. Astronauts experience a loss of bone tissue, which leads to backaches. Body fluid migration from the heart toward the brain causes blocked sinuses. The red blood cell count will fall, which leads to anemia. All these conditions are due to microgravity.

28. J

Space junk could collide with the spacecraft and damage it. This makes space travel dangerous for the astronauts. Space exploration makes a lot of space junk. Examples of space junk include used rocket boosters; old, unused satellites; and other materials, such as metals and solid fuel wastes.

29. Open Response

Statements 3 and 4 are valid statements explaining the importance for keeping accurate data in an experiment. While accurate data recording has no connection to other scientists conducting a similar experiment or varying the sample size, accurate data keeping does ensure that other scientist can conduct similar experiments to validate the results. Accurate data records can be used to prove or disprove the prediction made by the scientist.

30. G

Technology used in space shuttle fuel pumps has led to the development of better artificial hearts.

31. C

According to stories that are part of some traditional Aboriginal cultures, the moon was created and placed in the sky so that people could see during the night.

32. G

The Canadarm has never gathered samples from asteroids. The Canadarm has launched satellites, assisted in docking the space shuttle, and helped fix the Hubble Space Telescope.

33. B

The law of electrical charges states that like charges repel and unlike charges attract.
The tumbling action in a clothes dryer produced friction. The friction caused the electrons to leave one sweater and accumulate on another. The sweater that loses the electrons becomes positively charged while the sweater that gains the electrons becomes negatively charged. Unlike charges will attract, which is the reason the sweaters stick together.

34. H

On an electroscope, a charged object transfers its charge to the foil strips. A positively charged rod causes each foil strip to become positively charged. Positively charged objects repel each other. This causes the foil strips to move apart. This is caused by static electricity
In a compact disc player, current electricity runs the motor from an electrical plug-in or batteries, causing the disc to turn.

35. Open Response

Current electricity is used to make electrical power. Current electricity refers to the flow of electric charges in a circuit through a conductor in a controlled manner. An electric circuit is a continuous, looping path for electricity to flow through. Electricity flows along a conductor from an energy source, such as a battery, to a device that uses the energy, such as a light bulb. Static electricity cannot be used in this manner because it discharges randomly, while current electricity provides a continuous flow of electricity that devices need.

36. J

The water is slowed down by the beaver dam. The dam acts as resistance to the normal flow of the stream. Therefore, the water analogy refers to resistance in an electrical circuit.

37. A

All four diagrams show a complete electric circuit. To measure the potential difference across lamp A, the voltmeter must be connected in parallel with a circuit component. This is shown by diagram A.

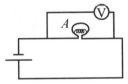

38. H

Sheldon should place the resistor at point Y in the circuit. This will not affect the current flowing through bulb 1, but it will reduce the current flowing through bulb 2.

39. C

The potential difference across the resistor of R ohms with a current of I amperes is calculated using $V = I \times R$. Therefore, the potential difference across the resistor is IR volts.

40. H

Efficiency is equal to the output energy of a device divided by the input energy of a device multiplied by 100. In this case, the calculation should read
Efficiency = 1 850 kJ / 2 250 kJ × 100
Efficiency = 82%

41. C

The electrical power entering your house must first be directed into the circuit breaker panel box. Beyond the panel box, it really does not make a difference whether the outlet or the light is wired next.

42. F

Tides and waves are used as an alternative method for generating electrical power. The motion of the incoming and outgoing tides turns the turbines connected to the generators.

43. C

The given diagram shows a parallel circuit. In this parallel circuit, each bulb is connected by a separate wire to form two separate pathways to the power source. Therefore, if one bulb is removed the electricity can still flow through the other bulb. Therefore, if bulb 2 were removed from this circuit, bulb 1 would remain on.